Spanish Verb HANDBOOK

Mike Zollo

Spanish Verb Handbook

The Author:

Mike Zollo is an experienced teacher, author and chief examiner. He is the chairman of the Association for Language Learning Spanish and Portuguese Committee.

The Series Editor:

Christopher Wightwick is a former UK representative on the Council of Europe Modern Languages Project and principal Inspector of Modern Languages for England.

Author's acknowledgement

I would like to thank Matilde Gutiérrez Manjón for her meticulous checking of the typescript and for some invaluable suggestions.

Other titles in the Berlitz Language Handbook Series:

French Grammar Handbook
German Grammar Handbook
Spanish Grammar Handbook
French Verb Handbook
German Verb Handbook
French Vocabulary Handbook ('94)
German Vocabulary Handbook ('94)
Spanish Vocabulary Handbook ('94)

Published by Berlitz Publishing Co., Ltd.,
Peterley Road, Oxford OX4 2TX, U.K.

1st printing 1993

Printed in the U.S.A.

CONTENTS

How to use this Handbook

This book aims to provide a full description of the Spanish verb system for all learners and users of the Spanish language. It provides the following information:

• a chapter explaining the Spanish verb system;
• the conjugation of 58 verbs, grouped to show the common patterns underlying the system;
• a subject index to *The verb system in Spanish*;
• a verb index, containing over 2,200 verbs with their English meanings and references to the pattern(s) they follow.

An important feature of the book is that examples, showing many of the verbs in use, are given throughout *The verb system in Spanish* and the *Model verbs*.

THE VERB SYSTEM IN SPANISH

Use the *Contents* and *Subject index* to find your way around this section, which describes the functions and forms of verbs in general. Information is given on the use of tenses, word order, the way verbs govern other parts of speech and the way verbs are formed. Methods of avoiding the passive are described, and features such as the reflexive forms, the subjunctive, **ser** and **estar** and the auxiliary verbs are explained. The main features of predictability and irregularity are explained, and key irregular verbs are illustrated.

MODEL VERBS

Use the *Verb index* to find your way around this section, which gives the full conjugation of one key model verb (**lavar**) in all of its active and passive forms and of every tense of the other verbs in their active forms. Models are provided for all three groups of regular verbs plus the full range of spelling-change and stem-changing verbs, followed by all useful irregular verbs. This makes 58 model verbs in total.

The conjugation of each verb is given in all usable tenses. Tenses which have any irregularity are given in full. For tenses which are predictable, and most especially for compound tenses, only the first person singular form is given, as this is sufficient to enable you to predict the remaining forms within those tenses. Therefore, if a tense is not given in full, you can assume that it is regular.

For simple tenses, just look at the first model verb (**lavar**) or at one of the three regular verb models (model verbs 2, 3 and 4) to figure out the endings needed. For compound tenses, check *The verb system in Spanish* to decide which tense of which auxiliary verb is necessary, then look up the appropriate auxiliary verb (**haber**, **estar** or **ser**) in the *Model verbs*.

Where appropriate, the model verb pages also contain the following.

• A list of other verbs following the same pattern. If possible, all such verbs are given. If, however, they are too numerous to list, a selection of the most useful ones is given. There are, of course, verbs which stand alone, having no others following their model.
• Notes indicating the main features of this pattern, and any variations or additional features affecting any of the verbs which basically follow that model.
• Short dialogues, narratives or sentences which illustrate some of the different tenses and usages of these verbs.

For further information on how the verb system works, refer to *The verb system in Spanish*.

SUBJECT INDEX

The *Subject index* gives section references for all of the main grammatical terms used in *The verb system in Spanish*.

VERB INDEX

For each of the 2,200 or so verbs listed, information is given on whether it is transitive (*tr*), intransitive (*intr*) or reflexive (*refl*), together with its English meaning. Common secondary meanings are also listed, as are the main idiomatic expressions based on common verbs. Finally, each entry is referred to the model verb whose pattern it follows.

* **jugar (a)** *(intr)* play; act out, play a part, play around; gamble **21**
jugar el papel de *(intr)* act out, play a role

There are verbs which have more than one predictable or unpredictable variation from the norm. Such verbs have two numbers after them and both model verb pages should be consulted in these cases.

HOW TO FIND THE INFORMATION YOU WANT

If you want to check on the form, meaning or use of a verb, first look it up in the *Verb index*. This shows:

• which verbs are model verbs (indicated by an asterisk);

* **abrir** *(tr/intr)* open, open out, open up **25**

• any preposition normally accompanying the verb;

echar la culpa a *(tr)* blame **2**

• whether the verb is transitive (*tr*), intransitive (*intr*) or reflexive (*refl*);

acabar *(tr)* finish, complete; accomplish **2**

• the main English meaning of the verb, along with any important idiomatic uses;

entregar *(tr)* deliver, hand over, hand in; turn over, yield **7**
entregarse a *(refl)* become addicted

• a number indicating the model verb which gives further information about the verb, how it is formed and others that follow a similar pattern.

absorber *(tr)* absorb **3**

If you want further information on the form or use of the verb, turn to the verb reference given.

A

THE VERB SYSTEM IN SPANISH

1 What verbs do

Note For more extensive treatment of the functions and uses of Spanish verbs, see the Berlitz *Spanish Grammar Handbook.*

1a *Full verbs*

The great majority of verbs tell us about the actions, state of mind or (possibly changing) situation of the subject of the sentence. These we call *full* verbs.

***Vivo* en una casa.**	I *live* in a house.
***Tenemos* un perro.**	*We have* a dog.

1b *Auxiliary verbs*

A much smaller group of verbs is used almost exclusively to add something to the sense of a full verb, for example to make a compound tense or to add a comment on an action. These are called *auxiliary* (helping) verbs.

***He* comprado una casa.**	*I have* bought a house.
***Suelo* ir a la oficina en coche.**	*I usually* go to the office by car.

1c *Dual-purpose verbs*

Some verbs can be used either with full meaning or as an auxiliary. For example, Spanish **estar** (to be), used mostly to express position or the state or condition of something or somebody, is also used as the auxiliary verb to form the present progressive/continuous tense: this describes an action actually in progress.

***Está* en la cocina.**	*She is* in the kitchen.
***Está* preparando la cena.**	*She is* preparing dinner.

2 What verbs govern

A sentence can contain many items of information other than what is given by the subject and the main verb. Some of these items depend directly on the main verb and cannot be removed without leaving the sentence incomplete. These items are said to be *governed* by the verb.

2a Lone verbs (intransitive verbs)

Some verbs do not normally govern an object [➤2c], though the sentence may, of course, contain adverbials which add to the meaning. These verbs are called *intransitive verbs* and are usually marked in verb lists and dictionaries as (intr).

***Estaban charlando* ruidosamente.**	*They were chatting* noisily.

They were chatting makes sense by itself. Although we know how they were chatting (noisily), this information is not necessary for the basic sense of the sentence.

2b Verbs linking equals: the complement

A small number of verbs simply act as a link between the subject and another word or phrase, which is called the *complement* of the verb. Usually the complement is a noun phrase, in which case it refers to the same person or thing as the subject.

Mi padre fue *profesor.*	My father was *a teacher.*

It can be seen that the noun phrase complement (**profesor**) refers to the subject (**mi padre**).

2c Verbs with one object (transitive verbs)

Many verbs take a *direct object* (i.e. the person or thing affected by the main verb). These verbs are *transitive*. They are usually marked in dictionaries and verb lists as (tr). A direct object answers the question *what?* or *whom?*. Intransitive verbs cannot have a direct object.

Mi amigo compró *un perro.*	My friend bought *a dog.*

Here, the dog was what my friend bought, so it is the direct object of *bought.*

2d Verbs which can be both transitive and intransitive

Many Spanish verbs can be used both transitively and intransitively, either standing alone or having an object. They may be listed as (tr/intr).

Mis amigos *hablaban* mucho, pero *hablaban español.*	My friends *were talking* a lot, but *they were speaking Spanish.*

2e Verbs with two objects: direct and indirect

Some transitive verbs describe the transfer of the direct object to another person (or possibly thing). This person is then the *indirect object* of the verb. The idea can be extended with some verbs to include people indirectly affected by the action of the verb. The indirect object answers the question *to whom?* or *for whom?*.

Siempre le da *diez pesetas al mendigo.*	He always gives *ten pesetas to the beggar.*

The money is the direct object, and the beggar – the beneficiary – is the indirect object.

2f Objects which refer to the subject: reflexive verbs

Another type of verb describes an action which 'rebounds' or 'reflects' on the subject, or – put another way – the subject and indirect object are one and the same. In English, they will often involve the use of one of the '-self' pronouns. These are called *reflexive verbs*; the vast majority of these verbs can be used as ordinary transitive verbs too (e.g. **lavar** (to wash); **lavarse** (wash oneself)). Many verbs are reflexive in Spanish which are not in English.

***Se está duchando* en el cuarto de baño.**	*He's having a shower* in the bathroom.
Todos los días, *se paseaba* por el parque.	Every day, *he used to go for a walk* in the park.
***Se lavó* las manos antes de comer.**	*He washed* his hands before eating.

2g *Verbs plus prepositions*

Many verbs, including those describing motion or situation, are supported by an adverb or a prepositional phrase.

Estamos *aquí.*	We are *here.*
Vive *en aquella casa.*	He lives *in that house.*

2h *Verbs governing verbs*

(i) *Verbs + infinitives*

This is a very common structure in Spanish, which has many expressions based on a modal auxiliary verb [➤3 below].

***Queremos salir* a las ocho.**	*We want to go out* at eight.
Me gusta* mucho *bailar.	*I like dancing* very much.
¿Sabes nadar?	*Can you swim?*

(ii) *Verbs + prepositions + infinitives*

Spanish also has a number of these structures, which are very similar to the above, but with a preposition between the auxiliary verb and the main verb.

***Vamos a cenar* en un restaurante.**	*We are going to dine* in a restaurant.

Acababan de llegar.	*They had just arrived.*
***Salió sin cerrar* la puerta.**	*She went out without shutting* the door.

(iii) *Verbs + participles*

(A) Verb + present participle: like English, Spanish has a way of describing an action in progress; this is done by using the verb **estar** (be) with the present participle, usually referred to by Spanish teachers as the *gerund.*

***Estábamos comiendo* cuando llegó.**	*We were eating* when he arrived.

(B) Verb + past participle: past events can be described by using the auxiliary verb **haber** with a past participle. In addition, **ser** plus a past participle is used to form the passive [➤9] and **estar** plus a past participle can be used to describe a state resulting from an action.

***Ha llegado* el capitán.**	The captain *has arrived.*
La nueva guía *será publicada* en mayo.	The new guide *will be published* in May.
La ventana *está rota.*	The window *is broken.*

2i Position of verbs in the sentence

(i) Generally speaking, the word order in a Spanish sentence is similar to that of a sentence in English; if anything, Spanish word order is slightly more flexible, but experience is more useful here than any hard-and-fast rules.

(ii) One important difference is that Spanish verbs are usually found without an accompanying subject pronoun [➤10a]. This is because each verb ending is clear and distinct, not just in the written but also in the spoken form. The verb endings themselves, therefore, convey the idea of person without the need for subject pronouns. The pronouns are, however, used for emphasis, contrast or to avoid ambiguity, when necessary.

¿Quién rompió la ventana?	Who broke the window?
–¡La rompió *él*, señor!	– *He* did it, sir!
Bueno, *yo* voy al teatro y *tú* vas al cine, ¿no es eso?	So, *I*'m going to the theater, and *you*'re going to the movies, right?
¿Tiene *usted* coche?	Do *you* have a car?

(iii) *Questions*

Questions are usually formed in English by inverting verb and subject (with or without auxiliary *do*), but in Spanish such inversion is not so common and is not, in any case, possible if there is no separate subject pronoun. Instead, questions are indicated by use of the inverted question mark at the beginning of the sentence in written Spanish, and by the question intonation pattern in spoken Spanish.

Mi madre tiene un coche nuevo.	My mother has a new car.
¿Tu madre tiene un coche nuevo? **¿Tiene tu madre un coche nuevo?**	Does your mother have a new car?
Tienes muchos amigos.	You have a lot of friends.
¿Tienes muchos discos?	Do you have many records?

(iv) *Negative expressions*

Negative expressions in Spanish are quite straightforward and have no effect on the position of the verb in the sentence. *No* and *not* are both translated by **no**, which is placed immediately before the verb and any dependent object pronouns.

Mi novio *no* va a la playa conmigo.	My boyfriend is *not* going to the beach with me.
¿Lo tienes tú? – No, *no* lo tengo.	Do you have it? – No, I do*n't* have it.
¿Has recibido la carta?	Have you received the letter?
– No, *no* la he recibido.	– No, I have*n't* received it.

No can be combined with other negative expressions (**nada**, **nunca**, **nadie**, etc.), placed around the verb.

***No* le dije *nada*.**	I said *nothing* to him.
***No* fuimos *nunca* a Bogotá.**	We *never* went to Bogotá.

***No* conocí a *nadie* en Las Vegas.**	I did*n't* meet *anyone* in Las Vegas.

Note **Nadie** (and sometimes **nada**) can begin a sentence, in which case there is no need for **no**. This does not affect the position of the verb in the sentence.

***Nadie* llama a la puerta.**	There is *nobody* at the door.
***Nada* tengo en el bolsillo.**	I have *nothing* in my pocket.

3 Attitudes to action: modal verbs

3a The function of modal verbs

Modal auxiliary verbs, as mentioned in 2h(i) above, modify full verbs to express an additional viewpoint such as possibility, desire or obligation. They are used in the appropriate person and tense form, followed by the infinitive of the full verb.

3b The verbs and their meanings

The following are the main modal auxiliary verbs used in Spanish.

(i) ***poder*** *be able, can*

No puedo **ir contigo.**	*I can't* go with you.

(ii) ***querer*** *want, wish*

La actriz no ***quería*** **decir más.**	The actress didn't *want* to say any more.

(iii) ***gustar*** *please*

This verb is used to express *to like.*

No le ***gustaba*** **bailar.**	He didn't *like* to dance/dancing.
¿Te ***gustaría*** **salir conmigo?**	*Would* you *like* to go out with me?

(iv) ***deber*** *have to, must, be obliged to, ought to*

¡No ***debes*** **hacer eso!**	You *must* not do that!
Deberían **escuchar al profesor.**	*They should/ought to* listen to the teacher.

(v) ***deber de*** *must*

This verb is used to express probability.

Debe de **estar ya en Buenos Aires.**	*He must* be in Buenos Aires by now.

(vi) ***tener que*** *have to, must, be obliged to*

Tenemos que **volver a casa.**	*We have to* go home.

(vii) ***dejar*** *allow, permit*

Mis padres no me *dejan* salir.	My parents won't *let* me go out.

(viii) ***permitir*** *permit, allow*

No se *permite* aparcar aquí.	Parking is not *allowed* here.

(ix) ***hacer*** *get something done, do, make*

Voy a *hacer* reparar mi coche.	I'm going to *get* my car fixed/repaired.

Note **Gustar** (and other verbs, such as **apetecer**) are known as impersonal or 'back-to-front' verbs. For more details on their use see Berlitz *Spanish Grammar Handbook*.

4 Verb forms not related to time

Verbs are very versatile words, in that a single verb form will usually give three pieces of information. As well as telling you *what* basic action or abstract verbal idea is referred to, it will tell you *who* is responsible and *when* it is happening. However, there are some verb forms which do not specify time or person.

4a *The infinitive*

The key part of the verb, as found in a verb list or dictionary – and indeed in the *Verb index* of this book – is the *infinitive*, and this only explains *what* is being described. In Spanish, the infinitive form of all verbs ends in one of the following: **-ar**, **-er**, **-ir** (for example **lav*ar***, **com*er***, **viv*ir***).

4b *The two participles*

(i) *The present participle*

This is a form of the verb often used to describe an action in progress; in Spanish, this is usually known as the *gerund*. The Spanish gerund form consists of the basic verb stem and the ending **-ando** (**-ar** verbs) or **-iendo** (**-er** and **-ir** verbs). Its most common use is with the auxiliary verb **estar**, to form the progressive/continuous tenses [➤6a(ii) and 6b(ii)], but it can also be used by itself, provided that its subject and that of the other verb in the sentence are the same.

La chica está *dibujando* un gato.	The girl is *drawing* a cat.
Estaban *jugando* cuando los vi.	They were *playing* when I saw them.
***Cruzando* la calle, vi un coche rojo.**	*Crossing* the street, I saw a red car.

Note Although the present participle is often referred to as the *gerund* in Spanish, it is important not to confuse this with the English gerund (the form which ends in '-ing'). The English gerund is often used in situations where Spanish uses an infinitive.

Me gusta *bailar*.	I like *dancing*.
Se prohibe *fumar*.	No *smoking*.

(ii) The past participle

This form is used to describe an action which is finished. In Spanish, it ends in **-ado** (**-ar** verbs) or **-ido** (**-er** and **-ir** verbs). [➤6b(iv) for irregular past participles.] It is very often used with the auxiliary verb **haber** to form the perfect tenses and other compound tenses, but it is often used in other ways, including as an adjective and to form the passive. When used with **haber** in compound tenses, it does *not* agree with either the object or the subject, but elsewhere it does.

Ha *salido* sin decir nada.	He has *gone out* without saying anything.
Estos son los cuadros *pintados* por Picasso.	These are the pictures *painted* by Picasso.
En la calle había unas botellas *rotas*.	In the street there were some *broken* bottles.
Esta casa fue *construida* por Mateos S.A.	This house was *built* by Mateos and Co.

Note In the four examples above, the past participle is used as part of a compound tense in the first, as an adjective in the second two and as part of a passive construction in the fourth.

In these last three examples, therefore, the past participles agree with the noun to which they relate, as this happens when the past participle is used as an adjective or is used to form the passive.

5 The passage of time and the use of tenses

5a *What do tenses tell us?*

'Tense' is not the same thing as 'time', though the same words are often used to refer to both. Time is a fact of life, in which there are only three time zones (past, present and future). Tenses, on the other hand, are grammatical structures which often reflect a way of looking at an event as well as just recording when it happened. Both the number of tenses and the names given to them vary from one language to another, though fortunately the main Spanish tenses correspond closely to those in English.

5b *One word or two? Simple and compound tenses*

Most verb forms consist of two parts: one describes *what* is going on; this basic part is called the *stem* or *root* of the verb, and for most tenses this is the infinitive minus the **-ar**, **-er** or **-ir** (for example, for the verbs **lavar**, **comer** and **vivir** these are **lav-**, **com-** and **viv-**); the other part defines *who* is responsible and *when* it is happening. There are two sorts of tenses: simple tenses and compound tenses.

(i) *Simple tenses*

These are formed by adding special sets of endings to a basic stem or root: the stem tells what the action or verb idea is, and the ending gives the *who* and *when* information.

(ii) *Compound tenses*

These use an auxiliary (helping) verb along with a special form of the main verb – a participle or the infinitive itself.

Thus, in the language of grammar, a simple tense is a one-word form, whilst a compound tense uses two or more words. Not counting the passive, in which all tenses are compound, Spanish has five simple tenses (seven including the subjunctive) and seven compound tenses (nine including the subjunctive). This is not as daunting as it seems, because some tenses are not often used, especially in speech, and so it will probably be enough simply to be able to recognize them when you hear or read Spanish. In any case, once you know how to use the auxiliary verbs **haber**, **ser** and **estar**, any compound tense can be formed by adding the appropriate participle.

Note The verb endings in Spanish are clear and distinctive in both written and spoken language, and so subject pronouns (the person words listed in 10a below) are not usually needed, since the verb endings themselves make it clear *who* is involved [➤2i(ii)].

5c *Auxiliary verbs used to form compound tenses*

The compound tenses in Spanish fall into two groups, each using a different auxiliary verb. They should both prove easy for English speakers to master, as the positive forms are composed in exactly the same way as their equivalents in English.

(i) The progressive/continuous tenses

These are used to describe actions which are in progress at the time being referred to. In English, these are easily identified, as they are formed by the appropriate form of the verb *be* followed by the main verb in the '-ing' form. Spanish uses an identical structure: the appropriate form of the verb **estar** followed by the gerund [➤4b(i)]. The two main tenses of this type are the present progressive/continuous and imperfect progressive/continuous: both describe an action in a more graphic, vivid way than their present and imperfect tense counterparts [➤6a(ii) and 6b(ii) below]. Note that Spanish uses the progressive/continuous tenses less than English, often preferring to use a simple tense.

¿No lo oyes? *Están cantando* en español.	Can't you hear? *They are singing* in Spanish.
Cuando me llamaste, *estaba planchando una camisa.*	When you called *I was ironing* a shirt.

(ii) The compound past tenses

In English, these tenses are formed with the appropriate form of the verb *have*. Again, Spanish uses an identical structure: the appropriate form of the verb **haber** followed by the past participle.

Note This is the only use of **haber** apart from the use of **hay**, **había**, etc. meaning *there is/are, there was/were*, etc. The verb **tener** is the verb normally used to convey the idea of possession.

¡*Ha llegado* Manuel!	Manuel *has arrived!*
***Habían visto* a Mariluz en la discoteca.**	*They had seen* Mariluz at the disco.

Note The past participle is also used in all passive forms [➤9 below].

6 Statements of probable fact: the indicative

Verb forms and tenses which make a positive statement are said to be *indicative*. [Contrast this with the subjunctive: ➤8.]

In all verbs there are some tenses whose stems and endings can be predicted if you know one of the other parts of the verb. Parts which cannot be predicted in this way have to be learned, but once these principal parts are known, it is usually possible to predict other parts. It is helpful to know how to obtain the stem, to which the endings for each tense are added, and any spelling adjustments that may need to be made. The following sections give a breakdown of the main uses of each tense, and explain how to get the stem and endings for each tense, along with any pitfalls to watch out for.

6a The present tense

The present tense in Spanish can be used to convey the following ideas.

- What the situation is *now*.

En este momento mi amigo *habla* con el profesor de inglés.	At the moment my friend *is talking* to the English teacher.

- What happens *sometimes* or *usually*.

En la clase de español, sólo *hablamos* español.	In the Spanish class, we only *speak* Spanish.

- What is going to happen *(quite) soon*.

Mañana me *voy* a Caracas.	Tomorrow I'm *going* to Caracas.

- What has been happening *up to now* and may be going to continue.

Llevamos **diez minutos *esperando.***	*We've been waiting* for ten minutes.
Estudio **español desde hace cuatro años.**	*I've been studying* Spanish for four years.

(i) The present indicative

This is formed by adding a set of endings to a stem, which consists of the infinitive with the **-ar**, **-er** or **-ir** ending removed.

comprar *(buy)*	***comer*** *(eat)*	***vivir*** *(live)*
compro	como	vivo
compras	comes	vives
compra	come	vive
compramos	comemos	vivimos
compráis	coméis	vivís
compran	comen	viven

Take care with all of the following [➤10b].

- Spelling-change verbs with changes to the final consonant of their stem ➤10b (ii).
- Stem-changing verbs (all groups) ➤10b (v)].
- Verbs whose first person singular stem ends in **-g-** (**poner**, etc.) ➤10b (vi).
- Verbs whose first person singular stem ends in **-zc-** (verbs in **-ocer**, **-ecer**, **-ucir**) ➤10b (vii).
- Verbs ending in **-uir** (**concluir**, etc.) ➤10b (iii).
- Verbs whose first person singular ends in **-oy** (**dar**, **estar**, **ir**, **ser**) ➤10b (viii).

For other irregular verbs, see *Model verbs*.

(ii) The present progressive/continuous

This is formed by using the present tense of **estar** plus the gerund [➤4b(i)].

comprar – comprando **comer – comiendo** **vivir – viviendo**

Note The following irregularities occur in the gerund.

- If the **-i-** of the ending comes between vowels, it becomes **-y**: **leer** (read) ➜ **leyendo**, **oír** (hear) ➜ **oyendo** and others [➤Model verbs 12,13].
- After **-ll-** and **-ñ-** the **-i-** is dropped: **zambullir** (dive) ➜ **zambullendo**, **gruñir** (grunt) ➜ **gruñendo**.
- The stressed vowel of some stem-changing verbs changes: **dormir** (sleep) ➜ **durmiendo**, **vestir** (dress) ➜ **vistiendo**, etc.

6b The past tenses

(i) The imperfect indicative

This is used for:
• repeated or habitual actions in the past;
• descriptions of things or people in the past;
• ongoing actions in the past, often as a setting or background to other actions.

Iba **a La Habana todos los años.**	*He used to go* to Havana every year.
Era **una pequeña casa blanca.**	*It was* a small white house.
Escribía **una carta cuando entré.**	*He was writing* a letter when I came in.

The imperfect indicative is formed by removing the infinitive ending and adding endings as follows.

compraba	comía	vivía
comprabas	comías	vivías
compraba	comía	vivía
comprábamos	comíamos	vivíamos
comprabais	comíais	vivíais
compraban	comían	vivían

Note The following verbs are irregular in the imperfect.

ser *(be)*	**ir** *(go)*
era	iba
eras	ibas
era	iba
éramos	íbamos
erais	ibais
eran	iban

Ver (see) retains the **-e-**: **veía**, etc.

(ii) The imperfect progressive/continuous

This is often used where a more vivid description of an ongoing action is needed. It is formed by using the appropriate imperfect tense form of **estar** followed by the gerund [➤5c(i) and compare ➤6a(ii)].

Cuando llegaste, yo *estaba planchando* mi camisa.	When you arrived, I *was ironing* my shirt.

(iii) The preterite

This is used for a single, completed action in the past, even if it spanned a long period, so long as the precise amount of time is defined.

***Compraron* este terreno el año pasado.**	*They bought* this land last year.
***Vivió* unos veinte años en Caracas.**	*She lived* for about twenty years in Caracas.

The preterite is formed by removing the infinitive ending and adding the endings shown below. Note the stressed endings in the first and third persons singular.

compré	comí	viví
compraste	comiste	viviste
compró	comió	vivió
compramos	comimos	vivimos
comprasteis	comisteis	vivisteis
compraron	comieron	vivieron

Note Watch out for the **pretérito grave** [➤10b (ix)], where the ending of the first and third persons singular is not stressed and the stem can be very irregular. Verbs of this type are marked *(pg)* in the *Model Verbs*. They include some very common verbs (**querer**, **tener**, **decir**, **poder**, etc.).

***tener** (have)*	***decir** (say)*
tuve	dije
tuviste	dijiste
tuvo	dijo
tuvimos	dijimos
tuvisteis	dijisteis
tuvieron	dijeron

There are further irregularities in the following types of verb, which should be checked in the relevant paragraph or section.

- Stem-changing verbs [➤10b (v)], types 2 and 3.
- Spelling-change verbs [➤10b(ii)].
- **Dar**, **ir**, **ser** [➤*Model verbs*].

• Verbs with the **-ieron** ending following a vowel, **-ll-** or **-ñ-** [➤*Model verbs*].

(iv) The rest of the past tenses in Spanish are compound tenses. They are formed using the appropriate tense of the auxiliary verb **haber** [➤*Model verbs*] and the past participle [➤4b (ii) and 6b (v)]. Note the following irregular past participles.

abrir	**abierto**	open
cubrir	**cubierto**	cover
descubrir	**descubierto**	discover, uncover
decir	**dicho**	say, tell
disolver	**disuelto**	dissolve
escribir	**escrito**	write
freír	**frito**	fry
hacer	**hecho**	make, do
poner	**puesto**	put
resolver	**resuelto**	solve, resolve
romper	**roto**	break
ver	**visto**	see
volver	**vuelto**	return

Note Compounds of these verbs have past participles with the same irregularities.

(v) The past participle is used with the appropriate tense of the auxiliary verb **haber** to form the following compound tenses, which largely correspond to their English equivalents.

(A) Perfect (present of **haber** + past participle)
The perfect is usually used to refer to an action which has recently taken place, much as in English, though the preterite can be used in much the same way.

Hemos terminado **el trabajo.**	*We have finished* the work.

(B) Pluperfect (imperfect of **haber** + past participle)
The pluperfect is used to take an extra step back from a time already in the past which is the focus of attention. It corresponds to the English *had . . .*

Habían hablado **con el médico.**	*They had spoken* to the doctor.

(C) Past anterior (preterite of **haber** + past participle)
The past anterior has the same meaning as the pluperfect, i.e. describing an action which *had taken place when . . .* It is used instead of the pluperfect after certain expressions and is fairly rare. See the Berlitz *Spanish Grammar Handbook* for further explanation.

Antes de que *hube salido*, llegó a casa.	Before *I went out*, he arrived home.

(D) Future perfect (future of **haber** + past participle)
The future perfect is used to take a step forward from a time in the past to express the idea of *will have . . .*

***Habrá comido* ya, y no querrá nada.**	*He will* already *have eaten*, and won't want anything.

(E) Conditional perfect (conditional of **haber** + past participle)

The conditional perfect is used to convey the idea of *would have . . .* and is often used to express something hypothetical or unfulfilled.

***Habríamos tomado el sol*, pero llovía.**	*We would have sunbathed*, but it was raining.

6c *The future tense*

In Spanish, the future can be conveyed in one of two ways: the *future immediate* and the *future simple*.

(i) *The future immediate*

This describes an action about to happen. It is formed by the appropriate part of the verb **ir** plus **a** plus the infinitive. The structure is very similar to its equivalent in English.

***Vamos a bañarnos* en el mar.**	*We are going for a swim* in the sea.
Este señor *va a volver* mañana.	This gentleman *is going to return* tomorrow.

(ii) The future simple

This is used for the following.

- Actions which are expected to happen in the future.

La semana que viene, *iremos* a Valparaíso.	Next week *we'll go* to Valparaíso.

- To express instructions.

Después de comer, *lavarás* los platos, ¿no?	After eating, *you'll wash* the dishes, won't you?

- To express predictions.

***Lloverá* esta tarde.**	*It will rain* this afternoon.

- To express probability.

***Tendrá* unos sesenta años.**	*He'll be* about sixty.

The future simple is formed by adding the appropriate set of endings to the *whole of the infinitive*. The only irregularity possible is in the stem, which always ends in **-r-** (see the irregular stems below). The endings are the same for all verbs. Note the stress accent on all the endings except **-emos**.

compraré	comeré	viviré
comprarás	comerás	vivirás
comprará	comerá	vivirá
compraremos	comeremos	viviremos
compraréis	comeréis	viviréis
comprarán	comerán	vivirán

Note The following stems are irregular.

caber	**cabré**	fit
decir	**diré**	say
haber	**habré**	have (auxiliary)
hacer	**haré**	do, make
poder	**podré**	be able
poner	**pondré**	put

querer	**querré**	want, love
saber	**sabré**	know
tener	**tendré**	have
valer	**valdré**	be worth
venir	**vendré**	come

and also compounds of any of these [➤10c].

6d *The conditional: What if?*

This is used – broadly speaking – for *would* or *should* (but not necessarily with the sense of obligation). In the actual expression of conditions, it is used to indicate the outcome rather than the condition itself, but it can also be used to express probability and the future in the past.

Me *gustaría comprarlos.*	I'*d like to buy them.*
Si tuviera dinero, *viviría* en San Francisco.	If he had the money, *he'd live* in San Francisco.
***Tendría* unos diez años cuando la vi por última vez.**	*She would have been* about ten when last I saw her.
Dijo que después de llegar, *llamaría* a su madre.	He said that after arriving *he would call* his mother.

The conditional has the same stem as the future [➤6c]. The endings are the same as the **-er/-ir** imperfect endings [➤6b(i)].

compraría	comería	viviría
comprarías	comerías	vivirías
compraría	comería	viviría
compraríamos	comeríamos	viviríamos
compraríais	comeríais	viviríais
comprarían	comerían	vivirían

Note The irregular future stems in 6c also apply to the conditional.

7 Requests and commands: the imperative

Orders and instructions can be given in a variety of ways.

- Expressing obligations.

***Tienes que* limpiar tu cuarto.**	*You have to* clean your room.

- Using the infinitive.

***Lavar* bien antes de comer.**	*Wash* well before eating.

- Using the imperative forms of the verb, as detailed below.

7a *The informal imperative positive singular*

The informal imperative positive singular (the **tú** form) is formed by removing the final **-s** from the second person singular of the present indicative.

compras → compra   comes → come   vives → vive

Note The following verbs have irregular forms:

decir	di	salir	sal
hacer	haz	ser	sé
ir	ve	tener	ten
poner	pon	venir	ven

¡*Compra* el mejor vino de España!	*Buy* the best wine of Spain!
¡*Sal* de ahí en seguida!	*Get out* of there at once!

Note also that pronouns can be attached to the end of positive imperatives, with the result that a written accent may be necessary to maintain the correct stress.

Dímelo.	Tell me (it).

7b The informal imperative positive plural

The informal imperative positive plural (the **vosotros** form) is formed by removing the **-r** of the infinitive and adding **-d**. There are no exceptions, but note that the **-d-** drops out when the reflexive pronoun **-os** is added. This is one of only three places where **-er** and **-ir** verbs have different endings.

comprar	comprad	lavarse	lavaos
comer	comed	ponerse	poneos
vivir	vivid	divertirse	divertíos

Note
- The accent on **-í-**
- **irse → idos** (go away)

***Comed* y *bebed* todo.**	*Eat* and *drink* it all.
***Ponedlos* en la mesa.**	*Put them* on the table.
***Sentáos*, chicos.**	*Sit down*, boys.

7c Informal negative imperatives and all formal imperatives

The negative informal imperatives (the **tú** and **vosotros** forms) and all the formal imperatives (the **usted** and **ustedes** forms) are formed using the present subjunctive. Informal imperatives use the second person endings and formal ones use the third person endings. Note that object pronouns *precede* the verb with negative imperatives.

Informal negative

no compres	no comas	no vivas
no compréis	no comáis	no viváis
no te laves	no te pongas	no te diviertas
no os lavéis	no os pongáis	no os divirtáis

Formal positive

compre Vd	coma Vd	viva Vd
compren Vds	coman Vds	vivan Vds

Formal negative

no compre Vd	no coma Vd	no viva Vd
no compren Vds	no coman Vds	no vivan Vds
no se lave Vd	no se ponga Vd	no se divierta Vd
no se laven Vds	no se pongan Vds	no se diviertan Vds

Any irregularity in the present subjunctive will, of course, occur in these imperatives [➤8].

Vuelvan **ustedes mañana.**	*Come back* tomorrow.
Póngase **este sombrero.**	*Put* this hat *on*.
Llévenlos **a casa.**	*Take them* home.
¡No *te caigas*!	Don't *fall*!
No las *comáis*.	Don't *eat* them.
¡No me *miren* así!	Don't *look at* me like that!
No *se sienten* allí.	Don't *sit* there.
No las *compre*.	Don't *buy* them.

7d Summary of imperative forms

	Informal		Formal
Positive singular (**tú**)	compra come vive	singular (**usted**)	compre coma viva
plural (**vosotros**)	comprad comed vivid	plural (**ustedes**)	compren coman vivan
Negative singular (**tú**)	no compres no comas no vivas	singular (**usted**)	no compre no coma no viva
plural (**vosotros**)	no compréis no comáis no viváis	plural (**ustedes**)	no compren no coman no vivan

8 Areas of uncertainty: the subjunctive

The subjunctive is used wherever a statement less than fact is made; often it is a case of doubt or uncertainty, or it is a case of an unfulfilled or hypothetical action. As explained in chapter 7, it is used extensively for many of the imperative forms. For more detailed explanation, see the Berlitz *Spanish Grammar Handbook*. By and large, the forms and tenses correspond to those of the indicative.

8a The present subjunctive

Stem: remove ending from first person singular present indicative.
Endings: the 'opposite' ones to the indicative, i.e. for **-ar** verbs endings begin with **-e-**, and for **-er** and **-ir** verbs endings begin with **-a-**.

compre	coma	viva
compres	comas	vivas
compre	coma	viva
compremos	comamos	vivamos
compréis	comáis	viváis
compren	coman	vivan

Note Watch out for the following.

- Stem-changing verbs of all types [➤10b(v)]. Pay particular attention to the further **e ➜ i** and **o ➜ u** changes in the second and third persons plural, types 2 and 3.
- Spelling changes to the final consonant of the stem [➤10b (ii)].
- Stems ending in **-g-** (**poner**, etc.) [➤10b (vi)].
- Stems with **-zc-** (verbs ending in **-ocer**, **-ecer**, **-ucir**) [➤10b (vii)].
- Verbs ending in **-uir** (**concluir**, etc.) [➤10b (iii)].
- Irregular present subjunctives: **caber ➜ quepa**, **haber ➜ haya**, **ir ➜ vaya**, **saber ➜ sepa**, **ser ➜ sea**. (For full sets of forms, see the *Model verbs*.)

No quiero que *comas* eso.	I don't want you to *eat* that.
Cuando *lleguemos*, tomaremos un café.	We'll have a coffee when *we arrive*.

8b *The imperfect subjunctive*

Stem: remove the ending from third person plural of the preterite. Endings: there are two forms of this tense, which are totally interchangeable except that the **-ra** forms alone can be used to replace the conditional. (See the Berlitz *Spanish Grammar Handbook* for detailed explanation.)

-ra forms

comprara	comiera	viviera
compraras	comieras	vivieras
comprara	comiera	viviera
compráramos	comiéramos	viviéramos
comprarais	comierais	vivierais
compraran	comieran	vivieran

-se forms

comprase	comiese	viviese
comprases	comieses	vivieses
comprase	comiese	viviese
comprásemos	comiésemos	viviésemos
compraseis	comieseis	vivieseis
comprasen	comiesen	viviesen

Any of the stem irregularities in the preterite (>6b (iii)) are carried right through both forms of the imperfect subjunctive.

mentir	**mintieron**	**mintiera/mintiese**	to lie
dormir	**durmieron**	**durmiera/durmiese**	to sleep
leer	**leyeron**	**leyera/leyese**	to read
decir	**dijeron**	**dijera/dijese**	to say
ir/ser	**fueron**	**fuera/fuese**	to go, be

Si *fuera* rico, me compraría un Ferrari.	If *I were* rich I'd buy a Ferrari.
Les dijo que se *callasen*.	He told them to *be quiet*.

8c *Compound subjunctive tenses*

The compound subjunctive tenses are formed by using the appropriate subjunctive tense of the auxiliary verb, followed by the past participle of the main verb, as can be seen clearly from the *Model verbs* [➤6b (iv) and (v)].

For further explanation, see the Berlitz *Spanish Grammar Handbook*.

9 Things done to you: the passive

9a *The true passive*

Used to express an action from the point of view of the 'victim', or the person/thing undergoing the action, the true passive is formed in the same way in Spanish as in English: use the appropriate part of the verb **ser** (be) followed by the past participle. (See *Model verbs* for complete conjugation of **ser**.) The only other thing to remember is that the past participle will have to agree in gender and number with the subject, as in the following examples.

La ventana *fue rota* por ese chico.	The window *was broken* by that boy.
Ramón *fue atropellado* por un camión.	Ramón *was run over* by a truck/lorry.
Mis hermanas *han sido vistas* por José.	My sisters *have been seen* by José.

9b *Alternatives to the true passive*

There are several ways of avoiding the true passive.

• Use the third person plural form of the verb impersonally.

***Me dicen* que va a llover.**	*I am told (they tell me)* that it is going to rain.
***Los robaron* ayer.**	*They were stolen* (*someone stole them*) yesterday.

• Turn the sentence upside down if there is an agent which you can turn into the subject.

Le mataron *los moros*.	He was killed by *the Moors* (*the Moors* killed him).

• Make the verb reflexive (this can only be done where the subject is inanimate).

La puerta *se cerró*.	The door *was closed* (*literally*: the door *closed itself*).
***Se cultiva* el arroz en la región de Valencia.**	Rice *is grown* (*literally*: *grows itself*) in the Valencia region.

- Use the redundant object pronoun.

La blusa *la* compró mi madre.	The blouse was bought by my mother (*literally*: the blouse – my mother bought *it*).

10 Types of Spanish verb

10a Predictability

The whole set of a verb's forms, including tense forms, is known as its *conjugation*. Within each tense in Spanish, there are six different forms of the verb, each one corresponding to a particular person as follows.

first person singular:	**yo**	I
second person singular:	**tú**	you (familiar)
	usted	you (formal)
third person singular:	**él**	he
	ella	she
first person plural:	**nosotros/as**	we
second person plural:	**vosotros/as**	you (familiar plural)
	ustedes	you (formal plural)
third person plural:	**ellos**	they (masculine)
	ellas	they (feminine)

Note *He*, *she* and *you* (formal singular) share the same verb form; *they* and *you* (formal plural) share the same verb form.

The various parts of the set of verb forms or conjugation are *predictable* at several levels.

(i) Regular verbs

Regular verbs are those for which you can predict any part of any tense from the spelling of the infinitive (plus of course a knowledge of the rules!). Infinitives in Spanish end in **-ar**, **-er** or **-ir** [➤4a], corresponding to the three main families of regular verbs, each with its own sets of forms and rules. Verbs in which some parts cannot be predicted in this way are *irregular*. Some of the commonest Spanish verbs are irregular.

(ii) Imports

Verbs brought into Spanish from other languages and newly coined verbs tend to be regular **-ar** type verbs.

dopar	dope, drug
esnifar	sniff (glue/solvents)
xerocopiar	photocopy

(iii) *Irregular verbs*

Some irregular verbs form groups, so if you know one you can predict the forms of any of the others. The so-called *stem-changing verbs* in Spanish fall into this category (**pienso**, **vuelvo**, **pido**, etc.).

There are also the following groups:

• those which have a **-g-** in the first person singular of the present indicative and therefore throughout the present subjunctive (e.g. **pongo**);
• verbs with **-zc-** in the same place (e.g. **conozco**) and therefore the same effect on the present subjunctive;
• verbs with the irregular **pretérito grave** [➤10b (ix)].

(iv) *Compound verbs*

With very few exceptions, compound verbs [➤10c] conjugate like their base verb. Thus, for example, **contener**, **detener**, **mantener**, **obtener**, **retener**, **sostener** all behave in the same way as their parent or base verb **tener**.

10b *Major groups of verbs: how are they conjugated?*

(i) *Conjugations*

There are three *conjugations* or groups of verbs in Spanish, which take a set of endings according to their infinitive [➤4a]. The infinitive ends in **-ar**, **-er** or **-ir**, and the regular or predictable members of each family [➤10a] behave in the same way, having the same sets of verb endings and methods of forming each tense. In fact, a look at the verb tables [➤*The complete system of tenses in Spanish* (Section B)] will show that, throughout the whole range of tenses, the endings for **-er** and **-ir** verbs are identical except for the following three endings which differ only in the vowel contained in the ending:

***-er* verbs** (e.g. **comer**)
present indicative: **comemos**, **coméis**
familiar plural imperative: **comed**

***-ir* verbs** (e.g. **vivir**)
present indicative: **vivimos**, **vivís**
familiar plural imperative: **vivid**

In all other tenses and persons they have identical endings.

(ii) Spelling-change verbs

These are verbs whose spelling has to be adjusted to maintain the correct consonant sound when the ending changes. This therefore only applies to the written language. The changes only apply to the last consonant(s) of the stem and fall into the following main categories:

-ar verbs: the following changes are necessary before **-e-** throughout the present subjunctive, and in the first person singular only of the preterite.

• Stem ends in **-c-** ➜ **-qu-**.
sacar (take out): **saque**, **saques**, etc; **saqué**
• Stem ends in **-z-** ➜ **-c-**.
empezar (begin): **empiece**, **empieces**, etc; **empecé**
• Stem ends in **-g-** ➜ **-gu-**.
pagar (pay): **pague**, **pagues**, etc; **pagué**
• Stem ends in **-gu-** ➜ **-gü-**.
averiguar (verify): **averigüe**, **averigües**, etc; **averigüé**

-er and **-ir** verbs: the following changes are necessary before **-o** in the first person singular of the present indicative, and before **-a-** throughout the present subjunctive.

• Stem ends in **-gu-** ➜ **-g-**.
seguir (follow): **sigo**; **siga**, **sigas**, etc.
• Stem ends in **-g-** ➜ **-j-**.
escoger (choose): **escojo**; **escoja**, **escojas**, etc.
• Stem ends in **-c-** ➜ **-z-**.
torcer (twist): **tuerzo**; **tuerza**, **tuerzas**, etc.

(iii) ***-uir*** *verbs*

Verbs ending in **-uir** have a **-y-** in the singular and third person plural of the present indicative, throughout the present and imperfect subjunctives, in the third person of the preterite and in the gerund.

concluir (conclude)

present indicative:	**concluyo**, **concluyes**, **concluye**, **concluimos**, **concluís**, **concluyen**.
present subjunctive:	**concluya**, **concluyas**, **concluya**, **concluyamos**, **concluyáis**, **concluyan**.
preterite:	**concluí**, **concluiste**, **concluyó**, **concluimos**, **concluisteis**, **concluyeron**.
imperfect subjunctive:	**concluyera/concluyese**.
gerund:	**concluyendo**.

Note This change also applies to all other verbs ending in **-uir**; **huir** (run away), **construir** (build), all verbs ending in **-struir**, **fluir** (flow) and verbs ending in **-fluir**.

(iv) Accents

A small number of verbs with a stem ending in **-i-** or **-u-** need an accent to stress this vowel in the singular and third person plural of the present.

enviar (send)
present indicative: **envío**, **envías**, **envía**, **enviamos**, **enviáis**, **envían**.
present subjunctive: **envíe**, **envíes**, **envíe**, **enviemos**, **enviéis**, **envíen**.
actuar (act)
present indicative: **actúo**, **actúas**, **actúa**, **actuamos**, **actuáis**, **actúan**.
present subjunctive: **actúe**, **actúes**, **actúe**, **actuemos**, **actuéis**, **actúen**.

Note **Desviar** (divert), **situar** (situate), **graduar** (grade) and **continuar** (continue) follow the same rules.

(v) Stem-changing verbs

The biggest group of not quite regular, but predictably irregular verbs in Spanish are those which are variously known as radical-changing, root-changing or stem-changing. In this book we refer to the part of the verb to which endings are added as the stem, so we shall use the term *stem-changing*.

You will probably have noticed that Spanish has many words containing the diphthong **-ue-** or **-ie-**, where corresponding or related words in other Latin languages, or even English, simply have **-o-** or **-e-**.

Spanish	*French*	*English*
puerto	port	port
muerto	mort	mortuary
siete	sept	septet
viento	vent	ventilation

This stem change often happens in Spanish when the original **-o-** or **-e-** is stressed. When a verb is conjugated, the stress varies from stem to ending according to the person and tense, and in some verbs the stem changes when stressed.

There are three main types of stem-changing verbs:

Type 1: **-ar** and **-er** verbs
Stem change: **e** to **ie**, **o** to **ue**, and **u** to **ue** (**jugar** only).
The changes occur only in the present indicative and subjunctive, where the stem is stressed, i.e. in all three singular forms and the third person plural.

pensar (think)
present indicative: **pienso**, **piensas**, **piensa**. . . **piensan**
present subjunctive: **piense**, **pienses**, **piense**. . . **piensen**

volver (return)
present indicative: **vuelvo**, **vuelves**, **vuelve**. . . **vuelven**
present subjunctive: **vuelva**, **vuelvas**, **vuelva**. . . **vuelvan**

jugar (play)
present indicative: **juego**, **juegas**, **juega**. . . **juegan**
present subjunctive: **juegue**, **juegues**, **juegue**. . . **jueguen**

Type 2: **-ir** verbs

Verbs of this type (e.g. **mentir** (lie), **dormir** (sleep) have the *same changes* in the *same places* as those of type 1, but additionally the stem vowel changes from **e** to **i** and **o** to **u** in the following.

gerund: **mintiendo**, **durmiendo** [➤4b (i)]

present subjunctive: the first and second persons plural [➤8a]
mintamos, **mintáis**; **durmamos**, **durmáis**

preterite: the third person singular and plural [➤6b (iii)]
mintió, **mintieron**; **durmió**, **durmieron**

imperfect subjunctive: throughout both forms of the imperfect subjunctive [➤8b]
mintiera/mintiese; **durmiera/durmiese**

Type 3: **-ir** verbs

Verbs of this type have the stem change in all the same places as type 2, but the change is *always* **e** to **i**.

pedir (request, ask for)
present indicative: **pido**, **pides**, **pide** . . . **piden**
present subjunctive: **pida**, **pidas**, **pida**, **pidamos**, **pidáis**, **pidan**
gerund: **pidiendo**
preterite: **pidió**, **pidieron**
imperfect subjunctive: **pidiera/pidiese**

(vi) *-g- verbs*

There is a group of verbs in which the stem of the present indicative contains **-g-** in the first person singular only, and therefore throughout the present subjunctive. Some have a perfectly regular present indicative except for the first person; others have stem changes [➤10b (v)].

hacer (do, make)
present indicative: **hago**, **haces**, **hace**, **hacemos**, **hacéis**, **hacen**
present subjunctive: **haga**, **hagas**, **haga**, **hagamos**, **hagáis**, **hagan**

tener (have)

present indicative:	**tengo**, **tienes**, **tiene**, **tenemos**, **tenéis**, **tienen**
present subjunctive:	**tenga**, **tengas**, **tenga**, **tengamos**, **tengáis**, **tengan**

The following verbs follow the same pattern.

caer (fall):	**caigo**, **caes**, etc.
poner (put):	**pongo**, **pones**, etc.
salir (go out):	**salgo**, **sales**, etc.
valer (be worth):	**valgo**, **vales**, etc.
decir (say):	**digo**, **dices**, **dice**, **decimos**, **decís**, **dicen**
oír (hear):	**oigo**, **oyes**, **oye**, **oímos**, **oís**, **oyen**

Note Both otherwise regular verbs and those containing stem changes keep the **-g-** stem unchanged throughout the present subjunctive.

(vii) ***-zc-*** *verbs*

Another sizeable group with an irregular first person singular in the present indicative consists of verbs whose infinitive ends in **-ecer**, **-ocer** and **-ucir**. The stem of the first person of the present indicative – and therefore all the present subjunctive – ends in **-zc-**.

parecer (seem)

present indicative:	**parezco**, **pareces**, **parece**, **parecemos**, **parecéis**, **parecen**
present subjunctive:	**parezca**, **parezcas**, **parezca**, **parezcamos**, **parezcáis**, **parezcan**

The following verbs follow the same pattern, as do many other verbs ending in **-ecer** and all other verbs ending in **-ducir**.

conocer	know	**lucir**	shine
reconocer	recognize	**conducir**	drive
aparecer	appear	**producir**	produce
desaparecer	disappear	**reproducir**	reproduce
ofrecer	offer	**traducir**	translate
merecer	deserve		

(viii) ***-oy*** *verbs*

In the following verbs, the first person singular present indicative ends in **-oy**. The present subjunctive is not affected by this.

dar (give):	**doy**, **das**, **da**, **damos**, **dais**, **dan**
estar (be):	**estoy**, **estás**, **está**, **estamos**, **estáis**, **están**

Note **Ir** (go) is irregular, but the present tense is quite predictable once established:

voy, **vas**, **va**, **vamos**, **vais**, **van**

(ix) Pretérito grave

A significant group of verbs have what is known as a **pretérito grave**: this refers to the fact that the first and third person singular preterite endings are not stressed and bear no accent; in addition, their set of preterite endings is a combination of the normal ones for **-ar** verbs (first and third person singular, but without accents), and **-er/-ir** verbs (all the rest).

tener (have): **tuve**, **tuviste**, **tuvo**, **tuvimos**, **tuvisteis**, **tuvieron**

The following verbs also have a **pretérito grave**.

andar	➜	**anduve**	**poner**	➜	**puse**
caber	➜	**cupe**	**querer**	➜	**quise**
estar	➜	**estuve**	**saber**	➜	**supe**
haber	➜	**hube**	**tener**	➜	**tuve**
hacer	➜	**hice**	**venir**	➜	**vine**
poder	➜	**pude**			

Note Watch out for the following.

- The third person singular of **hacer** is **hizo** in the preterite.
- When the stem of a **pretérito grave** ends in **-j-**, the third person plural ending is **-eron**.

decir	**dije**	**dijeron**
traer	**traje**	**trajeron**
conducir	**conduje**	**condujeron**

- Compounds of the above verbs follow the same pattern [➤10c]. So **componer** follows **poner**, **mantener** follows **tener**. Also, all verbs ending in **-ducir** follow the same pattern as **conducir**.

10c Compound verbs

A compound verb is one in which a prefix is added to the base verb. With very few exceptions, compound verbs conjugate in the same way as their base verb.

tener (have)	**tiene** (he has)
mantener (maintain)	**mantiene** (he maintains)

(i) Some compound verbs consist of a base verb with a prefix added which changes its meaning.

hacer (do, make)	➜	**deshacer** (undo)
	➜	**rehacer** (remake)
poner (put)	➜	**disponer** (dispose)
	➜	**componer** (compose)

Some common prefixes of this sort are listed below.

- **des-** which often corresponds to the English 'un-' or 'de-'.

atar (tie)	➜	**desatar** (untie)
congelar (freeze)	➜	**descongelar** (unfreeze, de-ice)
cubrir (cover)	➜	**descubrir** (discover, uncover)
hacer (do)	➜	**deshacer** (undo)

- **re-** is like the English or French 're-', but take care, as it is not used to the same extent to indicate repetition and is often used to intensify rather than repeat the action.

vender (sell)	➜	**revender** (resell)
llenar (fill)	➜	**rellenar** (fill up, fill out)
mojar (wet)	➜	**remojar** (soak, drench)
quemar (burn)	➜	**requemar** (scorch, parch)

- **mal-** gives the meaning of 'bad', 'badly' or 'evil'.

gastar (spend)	➜	**malgastar** (squander, waste)
decir (say)	➜	**maldecir** (curse)

Note The past participle of **maldecir** is **maldito**.

(ii) Other compound verbs are formed by the base verb having another part of speech added as a prefix.

contra (against) + **hacer** (do make)	= **contrahacer** (counterfeit, copy)
sobre (on, over) + **venir** (come)	= **sobrevenir** (happen unexpectedly)

(iii) Some common base verbs have a variety of prefixes.

- **Poner** (put) has compounds which often correspond to English verbs ending in '-pose'.

componer	compose; mend
descomponerse	decompose, rot; break down (machine)
deponer	depose, lay down (arms, etc.)
imponer	impose

interponer	interpose
posponer	put behind, postpone
proponer	propose, suggest
reponer	replace, put back; reply
suponer	suppose
presuponer	presuppose

• **Tener** (have) has compounds which correspond to English verbs ending in '-tain'.

contener	contain
detener	detain, stop
entretener	entertain, hold up, detain
mantener	maintain
retener	retain
sostener	sustain

• **Venir** (come) has a number of compounds.

convenir	agree, suit
intervenir	intervene
provenir	come forth
sobrevenir	happen, occur (unexpectedly)

• **Satisfacer** is a compound of **hacer** and behaves in the same way.

(iv) Sometimes the base verb does not exist: there are several verbs based on **-ducir**, corresponding to English verbs ending in '-duce' or '-duct', but there is no base verb **-ducir**.

conducir	conduct, lead, drive
deducir	deduce
inducir	induce, induct
introducir	introduce, insert
producir	produce
reducir	reduce
reproducir	reproduce
seducir	seduce
traducir	translate

11 Reflexive verbs

11a *Reflexive verbs in general*

See section 2f for a general explanation of reflexive verbs. In addition to the verbs which are reflexive in English, Spanish treats many other verbs as reflexive which are not in English. Many verbs can be used both reflexively and as ordinary transitive verbs.

11b *Reflexive pronouns*

The full set of reflexive pronouns accompanying these verbs can be seen in this example of the present tense of a reflexive verb.

lavarse	wash oneself
me lavo	I wash myself
te lavas	you wash yourself (informal)
se lava	(s)he washes her/himself, you wash yourself (formal)
nos lavamos	we wash ourselves
os laváis	you wash yourselves (informal)
se lavan	they wash themselves, you wash yourselves (formal)

11c *Position of reflexive pronouns*

Reflexive pronouns obey the same rules as other pronouns.

(A) They precede the verb:
• in all tenses of the indicative and the subjunctive;
• in all negative imperatives.

(B) They are joined to the end of the verb:
• in the gerund (optional);
• in all positive imperatives.

(C) With the infinitive, they can either precede the verb or be joined to the end of it.

Note The stress pattern may require the use of an accent to keep the stress on the same syllable.

¿*Te lavas* tú mismo ya, Paquito?	Do you already *wash* all by *yourself*, Paquito?
No *te peines* así.	Don't *comb* your hair like that.
Estoy *lavándome* ahora mismo.	I'm *washing* right now.
¡*Levántense* ahora mismo!	*Get up* immediately!
***Acuéstate* a las diez, ¿vale?**	*Go to bed* at ten, OK?
Vamos a *bañarnos* en seguida. / ***Nos* vamos a *bañar* en seguida.**	Let's *go for a swim* right now.

11d Use of the reflexive

Note that the reflexive form is often used where one would use a possessive adjective in English.

***Se lavaron las* manos.**	*They washed their* hands.
Mi novia *se pondrá el* vestido azul.	My girlfriend *will put on her* blue dress.

Note also the colloquial use of an apparent reflexive form to intensify a statement or request.

***Me comí* todas las manzanas.**	*I ate up* all the apples.

Note The reflexive is often used to avoid a true passive [➤9b].

B

MODEL VERBS

Index of model verbs

The complete system of tenses in Spanish

Regular verbs

Spelling-change verbs

Stem-changing verbs

Irregular verbs

Index of model verbs

Irregular verbs:		*Number*
abrir	open	25
adquirir	acquire	26
andar	walk	27
bendecir	bless	28
caber	fit; be contained	29
caer	fall	30
conducir	drive	31
conocer	know; get to know	32
dar	give	33
decir	say	34
erguirse	raise; lift	35
errar	wander; err	36
escribir	write	37
estar	be	38
freír	fry	39
haber	have (auxiliary)	40
hacer	do; make	41
ir	go	42
lucir	shine	43
oír	hear	44
oler	smell	45
poder	be able; can	46
poner	put	47
querer	want; love	48
reír	laugh	49
romper	break	50
saber	know	51
salir	go out	52
ser	be	53
tener	have	54
traer	bring	55
valer	be worth	56
venir	come	57
ver	see	58

1 lavar — wash

Regular **-ar** verb

GERUND	***PAST PARTICIPLE***
lavando	lavado

ACTIVE VOICE

PRESENT	***PERFECT***
lavo	he lavado
lavas	has lavado
lava	ha lavado
lavamos	hemos lavado
laváis	habéis lavado
lavan	han lavado

PRESENT PROGRESSIVE	***IMPERFECT PROGRESSIVE***
estoy lavando	estaba lavando
estás lavando	estabas lavando
está lavando	estaba lavando
estamos lavando	estábamos lavando
estáis lavando	estabais lavando
están lavando	estaban lavando

IMPERFECT	***PRETERITE***
lavaba	lavé
lavabas	lavaste
lavaba	lavó
lavábamos	lavamos
lavabais	lavasteis
lavaban	lavaron

PLUPERFECT	***PAST ANTERIOR***
había lavado	hube lavado
habías lavado	hubiste lavado
había lavado	hubo lavado
habíamos lavado	hubimos lavado
habíais lavado	hubisteis lavado
habían lavado	hubieron lavado

Notes ➤*The verb system in Spanish* for explanations of the tenses. The important thing to note here is that all forms have the basic part, or stem, **lav-**, which contains the meaning of the verb; many tenses are simple tenses, in which endings are added onto this stem to form just one word; other tenses are compound tenses, in which an auxiliary verb (helping verb) is used, in the appropriate tense and form, in front

IMPERATIVE

(tú) lava	(vosotros) lavad
(usted) lave	(ustedes) laven

FUTURE
lavaré
lavarás
lavará
lavaremos
lavaréis
lavarán

FUTURE PERFECT
habré lavado
habrás lavado
habrá lavado
habremos lavado
habréis lavado
habrán lavado

CONDITIONAL
lavaría
lavarías
lavaría
lavaríamos
lavaríais
lavarían

CONDITIONAL PERFECT
habría/hubiera lavado
habrías/hubieras lavado
habría/hubiera lavado
habríamos/hubiéramos lavado
habríais/hubierais lavado
habrían/hubieran lavado

PRESENT SUBJUNCTIVE
lave
laves
lave
lavemos
lavéis
laven

PERFECT SUBJUNCTIVE
haya lavado
hayas lavado
haya lavado
hayamos lavado
hayáis lavado
hayan lavado

IMPERFECT SUBJUNCTIVE
lavara/lavase
lavaras/lavases
lavara/lavase
laváramos/lavásemos
lavarais/lavaseis
lavaran/lavasen

PLUPERFECT SUBJUNCTIVE
hubiera/hubiese lavado
hubieras/hubieses lavado
hubiera/hubiese lavado
hubiéramos/hubiésemos lavado
hubierais/hubieseis lavado
hubieran/hubiesen lavado

of the appropriate gerund or participle of the verb which contains the meaning. Remember that, in Spanish, the subject pronoun (**yo** = I, **tú** = you, etc.) is not normally needed because the verb endings are so clear and distinct in both spoken and written forms; they are only needed for emphasis, contrast or to avoid ambiguity.

PASSIVE VOICE

For notes on other ways of expressing the passive ➤*The verb system in Spanish.*

PRESENT
soy lavado/a
eres lavado/a
es lavado/a
somos lavados/as
sois lavados/as
son lavados/as

PERFECT
he sido lavado/a
has sido lavado/a
ha sido lavado/a
hemos sido lavados/as
habéis sido lavados/as
han sido lavados/as

PRESENT PROGRESSIVE
estoy siendo lavado/a
estás siendo lavado/a
está siendo lavado/a
estamos siendo lavados/as
estáis siendo lavados/as
están siendo lavados/as

IMPERFECT PROGRESSIVE
estaba siendo lavado/a
estabas siendo lavado/a
estaba siendo lavado/a
estábamos siendo lavados/as
estabais siendo lavados/as
estaban siendo lavados/as

IMPERFECT
era lavado/a
eras lavado/a
era lavado/a
éramos lavados/as
erais lavados/as
eran lavados/as

PRETERITE
fui lavado/a
fuiste lavado/a
fue lavado/a
fuimos lavados/as
fuisteis lavados/as
fueron lavados/as

PLUPERFECT
había sido lavado/a
habías sido lavado/a
había sido lavado/a
habíamos sido lavados/as
habíais sido lavados/as
habían sido lavados/as

PAST ANTERIOR
hube sido lavado/a
hubiste sido lavado/a
hubo sido lavado/a
hubimos sido lavados/as
hubisteis sido lavados/as
hubieron sido lavados/as

¡Qué niño más sucio!
Madre Juan, *¿te estás lavando* o no?
Juan No, mamá, no me gusta *lavarme.*
Madre Pero, hijo, nunca *te lavas.* Deberías *lavarte* todos los días. ¿Cuándo *te lavaste* por última vez?

What a dirty boy!
Mother John, *are you washing,* or not?
John No, Mom, I don't like *washing.*
Mother But, son, *you* never *wash.* You should *wash* every day. When *did you* last *wash*?

FUTURE
seré lavado/a
serás lavado/a
será lavado/a
seremos lavados/as
seréis lavados/as
serán lavados/as

FUTURE PERFECT
habré sido lavado/a
habrás sido lavado/a
habrá sido lavado/a
habremos sido lavados/as
habréis sido lavados/as
habrán sido lavados/as

CONDITIONAL
sería lavado/a
serías lavado/a
sería lavado/a
seríamos lavados/as
seríais lavados/as
serían lavados/as

CONDITIONAL PERFECT
habría/hubiera sido lavado/a
habrías/hubieras sido lavado/a
habría/hubiera sido lavado/a
habríamos/hubiéramos sido lavados/as
habríais/hubierais sido lavados/as
habrían/hubieran sido lavados/as

PRESENT SUBJUNCTIVE
sea lavado/a
seas lavado/a
sea lavado/a
seamos lavados/as
seáis lavados/as
sean lavados/as

PERFECT SUBJUNCTIVE
haya lavado/a
hayas lavado/a
haya lavado/a
hayamos lavados/as
hayáis lavados/as
hayan lavados/as

IMPERFECT SUBJUNCTIVE
fuera/fuese lavado/a
fueras/fueses lavado/a
fuera/fuese lavado/a
fuéramos/fuésemos lavados/as
fuerais/fueseis lavados/as
fueran/fuesen lavados/as

PLUPERFECT SUBJUNCTIVE
hubiera/hubiese sido lavado/a
hubieras/hubieses sido lavado/a
hubiera/hubiese sido lavado/a
hubiéramos/hubiésemos sido lavados/as
hubierais/hubieseis sido lavados/as
hubieran/hubiesen sido lavados/as

Juan Hace dos días, y *me había lavado* dos días antes.
Madre Pero tus manos *deberían ser lavadas* varias veces al día, y tu cuello *debe ser lavado* por la mañana todos los días. ¡Vete a *lavarte* en seguida!

John Two days ago, and *I had washed* two days before.
Mother But your hands *should be washed* several times a day, and your neck *must be washed* every morning. Go and *wash* at once!

Regular **-ar** verb

GERUND	***PAST PARTICIPLE***
comprando	comprado

PRESENT	***PERFECT***
compro	he comprado
compras	has comprado
compra	ha comprado
compramos	hemos comprado
compráis	habéis comprado
compran	han comprado

PRESENT PROGRESSIVE	***IMPERFECT PROGRESSIVE***
estoy comprando	estaba comprando

IMPERFECT	***PRETERITE***
compraba	compré
comprabas	compraste
compraba	compró
comprábamos	compramos
comprabais	comprasteis
compraban	compraron

Notes The regular **-ar** verb conjugation is very large, so the verbs given below are only a small selection of the most useful verbs of this group. In the Verb Index the main meanings of each verb are given, and one or two can also be found in the reflexive form, sometimes with different meanings, e.g., **llamarse** 'to be called'; **echarse** 'to lie down'. Similarly, those used in reflexive form can often be used in non-reflexive form, e.g., **acostar** 'to put to bed'. Other verbs apparently in this group may be major irregular verbs, have minor spelling irregularities or be stem-changing verbs. For these you should consult the relevant section of this book. Note that some of the forms are quite similar to those of the **-er** and **-ir** verbs and that the following are the same:

- the first person singular (**yo**) ending in the present tense;
- the auxiliary verbs for the compound tenses;
- the formation and endings of the future tense.

Similar verbs

Only a very few of the most commonly used verbs are listed here.

ayudar	help	**dejar**	leave
bajar	go down	**entrar**	enter

IMPERATIVE

(tú) compra	(vosotros) comprad
(usted) compre	(ustedes) compren

PLUPERFECT
había comprado

PAST ANTERIOR
hube comprado

FUTURE
compraré

FUTURE PERFECT
habré comprado

CONDITIONAL
compraría

CONDITIONAL PERFECT
habría/hubiera comprado

PRESENT SUBJUNCTIVE
compre

PERFECT SUBJUNCTIVE
haya comprado

IMPERFECT SUBJUNCTIVE
comprara/comprase

PLUPERFECT SUBJUNCTIVE
hubiera/hubiese comprado

hablar	talk, speak	**mirar**	look
lavar	wash	**pasar**	pass (time)
llamar	call	**tomar**	take
llevar	carry, wear	**trabajar**	work

¡Qué ambicioso!
– ¿A qué hora *te levantas*?
– A las siete.
– ¿Por qué tan temprano?
– Quiero *llegar* temprano al trabajo.
– ¿Por qué?
– Para *ganar* mucho dinero. Un día voy a *comprarme* una casa muy grande, *pasaré* las vacaciones en América, y . . . ¡entonces me voy a *quedar* en la cama hasta mediodía! ¡Es por eso que ahora *trabajo* tanto!

What an ambitious chap!
"What time *do you get up*?"
"At seven."
"Why so early?"
"I want to *get to* work early."
"Why?"
"To *earn* lots of money. One day I am going to *buy* a very big house, *I shall spend* my vacations in America and . . . then I shall *stay* in bed until noon! That's why *I'm working* so hard now!"

Regular **-er** verb

GERUND	***PAST PARTICIPLE***
comiendo	comido

PRESENT	***PERFECT***
como	he comido
comes	has comido
come	ha comido
comemos	hemos comido
coméis	habéis comido
comen	han comido

PRESENT PROGRESSIVE	***IMPERFECT PROGRESSIVE***
estoy comiendo	estaba comiendo

IMPERFECT	***PRETERITE***
comía	comí
comías	comiste
comía	comió
comíamos	comimos
comíais	comisteis
comían	comieron

Similar verbs

Only some of the most commonly used verbs are listed here.

aprender	learn	**sorprender**	surprise
beber	drink	**suceder**	succeed, happen
correr	run	**temer**	fear
coser	sew	**toser**	cough
deber	owe, must	**vender**	sell
prometer	promise		

Notes Although the **-er** group of verbs is a large one, many verbs in this conjugation are irregular or are subject to spelling changes. These appear in the appropriate sections of this book, though those appearing above are examples of those which are entirely regular. Many of these verbs can be used in both reflexive and non-reflexive form; the most commonly used form is given in the above list. Note that some of the forms are very similar to those of the **-ar** verbs and that the following are the same as for both **-ar** and **-ir** verbs:

- the first person singular (**yo**) ending in the present tense;
- the auxiliary verbs for the compound tenses;
- the formation and endings of the future tense.

IMPERATIVE

(tú) come	(vosotros) comed
(usted) coma	(ustedes) coman

PLUPERFECT
había comido

PAST ANTERIOR
hube comido

FUTURE
comeré

FUTURE PERFECT
habré comido

CONDITIONAL
comería

CONDITIONAL PERFECT
habría/hubiera comido

PRESENT SUBJUNCTIVE
coma

PERFECT SUBJUNCTIVE
haya comido

IMPERFECT SUBJUNCTIVE
comprara/comprase

PLUPERFECT SUBJUNCTIVE
hubiera/hubiese comido

The following are the same as for **-ir** verbs:
- four out of six of the present tense forms;
- the gerund (or present participle) and the past participle;
- the preterite and imperfect.

¡Qué alumno más malo!
– ¿Qué le *sucede* a Sánchez? ¡*Parece* no *aprender* nada!
– Es que pasa todo su tiempo libre *vendiendo* periódicos en la calle. Le gusta *beber*, por eso *debe* ganar dinero . . .
– Ayer, Sánchez *prometió* que, de aquí en adelante, *aprenderá* todo muy bien.
– Espero qu sí. Si no, *temo* que *corre* el ríesgo de *suspender* sus exámenes.

What an awful pupil!
"What*'s happening* to Sánchez? He *seems to learn* nothing!"
"He's spending all his free time *selling* newspapers in the street. He likes *drinking*, so he *has to* earn money . . ."
"Yesterday, Sánchez *promised* that, from now on, *he will learn* everything well."
"I hope so. If not, *I fear he runs* the risk of *failing* his exams."

4 vivir — live

Regular **-ir** verb

GERUND	***PAST PARTICIPLE***
viviendo	vivido

PRESENT
vivo
vives
vive
vivimos
vivís
viven

PERFECT
he vivido
has vivido
ha vivido
hemos vivido
habéis vivido
han vivido

PRESENT PROGRESSIVE
estoy viviendo

IMPERFECT PROGRESSIVE
estaba viviendo

IMPERFECT
vivía
vivías
vivía
vivíamos
vivíais
vivían

PRETERITE
viví
viviste
vivió
vivimos
vivisteis
vivieron

Similar verbs

Only some of the most commonly used verbs are listed here.

aburrir	bore	**dividir**	divide
asistir	attend, assist	**partir**	depart, split
consistir	consist	**persuadir**	persuade
convivir	live together, coexist	**sobrevivir**	survive
decidir	decide	**subir**	go up, raise
discutir	discuss	**sufrir**	suffer
distinguir	distinguish	**unir**	unite

Notes The **-ir** group of verbs is a very large one, but many of its member verbs are irregular or are subject to spelling changes. These appear in the appropriate sections of this book, and those listed above are examples of those which are entirely regular. Many of these verbs can be used in both reflexive and non-reflexive forms; the most commonly used forms are given in the above list. Note that some of the forms are similar to or the same as those of the **-ar** and **-er** verbs. The following are the same as for both **-ar** and **-er** verbs:

- the first person singular (**yo**) ending in the present tense;
- the auxiliary verbs for the compound tenses;
- the formation and endings of the future tense.

IMPERATIVE

(tú) vive
(usted) viva
(vosotros) vivid
(ustedes) vivan

PLUPERFECT
había vivido

PAST ANTERIOR
hube vivido

FUTURE
viviré

FUTURE PERFECT
habré vivido

CONDITIONAL
viviría

CONDITIONAL PERFECT
habría/hubiera vivido

PRESENT SUBJUNCTIVE
viva

PERFECT SUBJUNCTIVE
haya vivido

IMPERFECT SUBJUNCTIVE
viviera/viviese

PLUPERFECT SUBJUNCTIVE
hubiera/hubiese vivido

The following are the same as for **-er** verbs:
- four out of six of the present tense forms;
- the gerund (or present participle) and the past participle;
- the preterite and imperfect tenses.

¡Qué tío más aburrido!
Tomás es un joven que *se aburre* muy fácilmente. Sus amigos *sufren* mucho, porque en lugar de *unirles* a todos con su amistad, les *divide* con su falta de interés. Cuando *se reúnen* todos para *decidir* qué van a hacer, no quiere *admitir* ninguna sugerencia. No sé cómo *sobreviven* sus amigos. Sin duda, al *morir*, ¡*subirán* directamente al cielo!

What a boring lad!
Thomas is a young man who *gets bored* very easily. His friends *suffer* a lot, because instead of *uniting them* all with his friendship, he *divides* them with his lack of interest. When *they* all *meet* to *decide* what to do, he won't *accept* any suggestion. I don't know how his friends *survive*. Without doubt, when *they die they will go* straight *up* to heaven!

5 sacar — take out

-ar verbs: **c → qu**

GERUND	*PAST PARTICIPLE*
sacando	sacado

PRESENT
saco

PRESENT PROGRESSIVE
estoy sacando

IMPERFECT
sacaba

PLUPERFECT
había sacado

PERFECT
he sacado

IMPERFECT PROGRESSIVE
estaba sacando

PRETERITE
saqué
sacaste
sacó
sacamos
sacasteis
sacaron

PAST ANTERIOR
hube sacado

Similar verbs

aparcar	park	**atracar**	assault, mug
aplicar	apply	**buscar**	look for, search
arrancar	start up	**confiscar**	confiscate
atacar	attack	**criticar**	criticize
tocar	touch, play *(instrument)*		

Notes The **-c-** changes to **-qu-** before verb endings beginning with an **-e-** in order to preserve the sound. In all other respects these verbs are regular. There are verbs other than those above which have the **c → qu** change, but they are also stem-changing verbs.

IMPERATIVE

(tú) saca
(usted) saque
(vosotros) sacad
(ustedes) saquen

FUTURE
sacaré

FUTURE PERFECT
habré sacado

CONDITIONAL
sacaría

CONDITIONAL PERFECT
habría/hubiera sacado

PRESENT SUBJUNCTIVE
saque
saques
saque
saquemos
saquéis
saquen

PERFECT SUBJUNCTIVE
haya sacado

IMPERFECT SUBJUNCTIVE
sacara/sacase

PLUPERFECT SUBJUNCTIVE
hubiera/hubiese sacado

El atraco
El sábado pasado, fui víctima de un atraco . . . Al llegar al centro ciudad, *busqué* un sitio para dejar el coche. Por fin *aparqué* en una calle oscura. Cuando bajé del coche, alguien me *tocó* en la espalda – con una navaja. El atracador me dijo – "*Saque* el monadero." En lugar del monedero, *saqué* mi alarma personal. Con el ruido, *el hombre que me atacó* se fue corriendo, y *volcó* un puesto de fruta al doblar la esquina. Un policía le detuvo, y *confiscó* la navaja.

The mugging
Last Saturday I was the victim of a mugging . . . When I got to the town center, *I looked for* somewhere to park the car. In the end *I parked* on a dark street. As I got out of the car, someone *touched* me in the back – with a knife. The mugger said, "*Get* your wallet *out.*" Instead of the wallet, *I took out* my personal alarm. With the noise *the attacker* ran off and *overturned* a fruit stand as he turned the corner. A policeman stopped him and *confiscated* the knife.

6 cazar hunt

-ar verbs: **z → c**

GERUND
cazando

PAST PARTICIPLE
cazado

PRESENT
cazo

PRESENT PROGRESSIVE
estoy cazando

IMPERFECT
cazaba

PLUPERFECT
había cazado

PERFECT
he cazado

IMPERFECT PROGRESSIVE
estaba cazando

PRETERITE
cacé
cazaste
cazó
cazamos
cazasteis
cazaron

PAST ANTERIOR
hube cazado

Similar verbs

abrazar	hug, embrace	**lanzar**	launch, throw
avergonzarse	be ashamed	**rezar**	pray

Notes The **-z-** changes to **-c-** before verb endings beginning with an **-e-**. In all other respects these verbs are regular. There are quite a few verbs other than those listed above which have the **z → c** change, but they are also stem-changing verbs.

El almuerzo del domingo
Hoy, domingo, *almorzamos* la familia y yo como siempre, pero, ¡qué desastre! Primero, *empecé* a comer antes que mi padre, así que se enfadó conmigo. Luego mi madre me dio espinacas

Sunday lunch
Today, Sunday, my family and I *had lunch* as usual, but what a disaster! First, *I started* to eat before my father, so he got annoyed with me. Then my mother gave me spinach . . .

IMPERATIVE

(tú) caza
(usted) cace
(vosotros) cazad
(ustedes) cacen

FUTURE

cazaré

FUTURE PERFECT

habré cazado

CONDITIONAL

cazaría

CONDITIONAL PERFECT

habría/hubiera cazado

PRESENT SUBJUNCTIVE

cace
caces
cace
cacemos
cacéis
cacen

PERFECT SUBJUNCTIVE

haya cazado

IMPERFECT SUBJUNCTIVE

cazara/cazase

PLUPERFECT SUBJUNCTIVE

hubiera/hubiese cazado

. . . me *esforcé* en comerlas pero, ¡qué asco! Mi madre también le *forzó* a mi hermano a comer patatas, y éste *comenzó* a gritar que no le gustaban . . . Por fin, papá *tropezó* al traer el postre, de manera que no tomamos postre. ¡Luego todos *empezamos* a gritar! ¡Espero que *reces* por nosotros y por la paz en nuestra familia!

I *made an effort* to eat it, but how disgusting! My mother also *forced* my brother to eat potatoes, and he *began* to shout that he didn't like them. . . Finally, Dad *tripped* when he brought in the dessert, so we had none. Then *we* all *began* to shout. I hope *you'll pray* for us and for peace in our family!

7 pagar pay

-ar verbs: **g ➜ gu**

GERUND	*PAST PARTICIPLE*
pagando	pagado

PRESENT
pago

PERFECT
he pagado

PRESENT PROGRESSIVE
estoy pagando

IMPERFECT PROGRESSIVE
estaba pagando

IMPERFECT
pagaba

PRETERITE
pagué
pagaste
pagó
pagamos
pagasteis
pagaron

PLUPERFECT
había pagado

PAST ANTERIOR
hube pagado

Similar verbs

apagar	put out, switch off	**obligar**	oblige
llegar	arrive		

Notes The **-g-** changes to **-gu-** before verb endings beginning with **-e-** in order to preserve the sound. In all other respects these verbs are regular. There are quite a few verbs other than those listed above which have the **g ➜ gu** change, but are also stem-changing verbs.

IMPERATIVE

(tú) paga
(usted) pague

(vosotros) pagad
(ustedes) paguen

FUTURE

pagaré

FUTURE PERFECT

habré pagado

CONDITIONAL

pagaría

CONDITIONAL PERFECT

habría/hubiera pagado

PRESENT SUBJUNCTIVE

pague
pagues
pague
paguemos
paguéis
paguen

PERFECT SUBJUNCTIVE

haya pagado

IMPERFECT SUBJUNCTIVE

pagara/pagase

PLUPERFECT SUBJUNCTIVE

hubiera/hubiese pagado

Instrucciones y publicidad	**Instructions and advertisements**
***Descuelgue* el receptor antes de marcar el número deseado.**	*Pick up* the receiver before dialling the number required.
¡*Friegue* sus platos con Flush!	*Wash* your dishes with Flush!
No *llegues* tarde – ¡compra un SEAT!	Don't *arrive* late – buy a SEAT!
¡No lo *niegues*, mis tomates son enormes! ¡Los *regué* con Bioriego!	Don't *deny* it, my tomatoes are enormous! *I watered* them with Bioriego!

8 averiguar — verify; check

-ar verbs: **gu → gü**

GERUND	*PAST PARTICIPLE*
averiguando	averiguado

PRESENT
averiguo

PERFECT
he averiguado

PRESENT PROGRESSIVE
estoy averiguando

IMPERFECT PROGRESSIVE
estaba averiguando

IMPERFECT
averiguaba

PRETERITE
averigüé
averiguaste
averiguó
averiguamos
averiguasteis
averiguaron

PLUPERFECT
había averiguado

PAST ANTERIOR
hube averiguado

Similar verbs

amortiguar	deaden, muffle	**apaciguar**	pacify, appease

Notes The **-gu-** changes to **-gü-** before verb endings beginning with an **-e-** in order to preserve the sound. In all other respects these verbs are regular.

IMPERATIVE

(tú) averigua
(usted) averigüe
(vosotros) averiguad
(ustedes) averigüen

FUTURE

averiguaré

FUTURE PERFECT

habré averiguado

CONDITIONAL

averiguaría

CONDITIONAL PERFECT

habría/hubiera averiguado

PRESENT SUBJUNCTIVE

averigüe
averigües
averigüe
averigüemos
averigüéis
averigüen

PERFECT SUBJUNCTIVE

haya averiguado

IMPERFECT SUBJUNCTIVE

averiguara/averiguase

PLUPERFECT SUBJUNCTIVE

hubiera/hubiese averiguado

Eso es todo lo que pude *averiguar*.	That's all I could *find out*.
¡*Averígualo* tú mismo!	*Find out* for yourself!
***Averígüelo* usted, por favor.**	Would you *find out*, please?

-er and **-ir** verbs: **c → z**

GERUND	***PAST PARTICIPLE***
venciendo	vencido

PRESENT
venzo
vences
vence
vencemos
vencéis
vencen

PERFECT
he vencido

PRESENT PROGRESSIVE
estoy venciendo

IMPERFECT PROGRESSIVE
estaba venciendo

IMPERFECT
vencía

PRETERITE
vencí

PLUPERFECT
había vencido

PAST ANTERIOR
hube vencido

Similar verbs

convencer	convince	**esparcir**	scatter, spread
ejercer	exercise	**mecer**	rock

Notes The **-c-** changes to **-z-** before verb endings beginning with an **-a-** or an **-o-** in order to preserve the sound. In all other respects these verbs are regular. There are verbs other than those listed above which have the **c → z** change, but they are also stem-changing verbs.

IMPERATIVE

(tú) vence | (vosotros) venced
(usted) venza | (ustedes) venzan

FUTURE
venceré

FUTURE PERFECT
habré vencido

CONDITIONAL
vencería

CONDITIONAL PERFECT
habría/hubiera vencido

PRESENT SUBJUNCTIVE
venza
venzas
venza
venzamos
venzáis
venzan

PERFECT SUBJUNCTIVE
haya vencido

IMPERFECT SUBJUNCTIVE
venciera/venciese

PLUPERFECT SUBJUNCTIVE
hubiera/hubiese vencido

No me *convences* . . .	*You* don't *convince* me . . .
¿Que no te *convenzo*?	So, *I* don't *convince* you?
¡*Convénzanos* a todos!	*Convince* all of us!
No nos *convencemos* fácilmente.	*We are* not easily *convinced.*
Al final de la calle, *tuerce* a la derecha.	At the end of the street, *turn* right.
No *tuerzas* a la izquierda.	Don't *turn* left.

-er and **-ir** verbs: **gu → g**

GERUND	*PAST PARTICIPLE*
distinguiendo	distinguido

PRESENT
distingo
distingues
distingue
distinguimos
distinguís
distinguen

PERFECT
he distinguido

PRESENT PROGRESSIVE
estoy distinguiendo

IMPERFECT PROGRESSIVE
estaba distinguiendo

IMPERFECT
distinguía

PRETERITE
distinguí

PLUPERFECT
había distinguido

PAST ANTERIOR
hube distinguido

Similar verbs

extinguir extinguish, put out

Notes The **-gu-** changes to **-g-** before verb endings beginning with an **-o-** or an **-a-**. In all other respects these verbs are regular. There are verbs other than **distinguir** and **extinguir** which have the **g → gu** change, but they are also stem-changing verbs.

IMPERATIVE

(tú) distingue
(usted) distinga
(vosotros) distinguid
(ustedes) distingan

FUTURE

distinguiré

FUTURE PERFECT

habré distinguido

CONDITIONAL

distinguiría

CONDITIONAL PERFECT

habría/hubiera distinguido

PRESENT SUBJUNCTIVE

distinga
distingas
distinga
distingamos
distingáis
distingan

PERFECT SUBJUNCTIVE

haya distinguido

IMPERFECT SUBJUNCTIVE

distinguiera/distinguiese

PLUPERFECT SUBJUNCTIVE

hubiera/hubiese distinguido

Hace falta que *distingas* entre los dos.	*You* need to *distinguish* between them.
¡*Persíguelo* y acaba con él!	*Chase him* and finish him off!
Mi amigo *consiguió* hacerlo.	My friend *managed* to do it.
Hace falta que *consigas* un diez.	*You* need to *get* ten out of ten.

-er and **-ir** verbs: **g → j**

GERUND	***PAST PARTICIPLE***
cogiendo	cogido

PRESENT
cojo
coges
coge
cogemos
cogéis
cogen

PERFECT
he cogido

PRESENT PROGRESSIVE
estoy cogiendo

IMPERFECT PROGRESSIVE
estaba cogiendo

IMPERFECT
cogía

PRETERITE
cogí

PLUPERFECT
había cogido

PAST ANTERIOR
hube cogido

Similar verbs

acoger	welcome	**proteger**	protect
escoger	choose	**restringir**	restrict
fingir	feign, pretend		

Notes The **-g-** changes to **-j-** before verb endings beginning with an **-a-** or an **-o-** in order to preserve the sound. In all other respects these verbs are regular. There are verbs other than those listed above which have the **g → j** change, but they are also stem-changing verbs.

IMPERATIVE
(tú) coge
(usted) coja
(vosotros) coged
(ustedes) cojan

FUTURE
cogeré

FUTURE PERFECT
habré cogido

CONDITIONAL
cogería

CONDITIONAL PERFECT
habría/hubiera cogido

PRESENT SUBJUNCTIVE
coja
cojas
coja
cojamos
cojáis
cojan

PERFECT SUBJUNCTIVE
haya cogido

IMPERFECT SUBJUNCTIVE
cogiera/cogiese

PLUPERFECT SUBJUNCTIVE
hubiera/hubiese cogido

Publicidad
¡Para perfeccionar su ortografía, *elija* Grafolín, el mejor bolígrafo de todos!

Advertisements
To perfect your handwriting, *choose* a Grafolín ballpoint, the best ballpoint of all!

Oración
¡Que Dios me *proteja* del mal! *Protégeme*, Señor . . .

Prayer
May God *protect* me from evil! Lord, *protect* me . . .

Impaciencia
¡Vamos, de prisa, *coja* esto!

Impatience
Come on, quickly, *grab* this!

12 huir — run away, flee

-uir verbs: **i → y**

GERUND
huyendo

PAST PARTICIPLE
huido

PRESENT
huyo
huyes
huye
huimos
huís
huyen

PERFECT
he huido

PRESENT PROGRESSIVE
estoy huyendo

IMPERFECT PROGRESSIVE
estaba huyendo

IMPERFECT
huía

PRETERITE
huí
huiste
huyó
huimos
huisteis
huyeron

Similar verbs

concluir	conclude	**disminuir**	diminish
construir	build, construct	**excluir**	exclude
destruir	destroy	**incluir**	include
distribuir	distribute	**influir**	influence

Notes The **-i-** is replaced by **-y-** to avoid three vowels coming together. In all other respects these verbs are regular.

IMPERATIVE

(tú) huye
(usted) huya

(vosotros) huid
(ustedes) huyan

PLUPERFECT

había huido

PAST ANTERIOR

hube huido

FUTURE

huiré

FUTURE PERFECT

habré huido

CONDITIONAL

huiría

CONDITIONAL PERFECT

habría/hubiera huido

PRESENT SUBJUNCTIVE

huya
huyas
huya
huyamos
huyáis
huyan

PERFECT SUBJUNCTIVE

haya huido

IMPERFECT SUBJUNCTIVE

huyera/huyese

PLUPERFECT SUBJUNCTIVE

hubiera/hubiese huido

¡*Huye*, que ya viene el profesor!	*Run*, teacher's coming!
Te digo que no *huyas* . . .	Don't *run away*, I tell you . . .
Los moros *construyeron* esta casa.	The Moors *built* this house.

-eer verbs: take a **-y-** between vowels

GERUND	***PAST PARTICIPLE***
leyendo	leído

PRESENT
leo

PERFECT
he leído

PRESENT PROGRESSIVE
estoy leyendo

IMPERFECT PROGRESSIVE
estaba leyendo

IMPERFECT
leía

PRETERITE
leí
leíste
leyó
leímos
leísteis
leyeron

PLUPERFECT
había leído

PAST ANTERIOR
hube leído

Similar verbs

creer	believe	**poseer**	possess

Notes The **-i-** is replaced by **-y-** to avoid three vowels coming together in certain forms (including the imperfect subjunctive), and in others the **-i-** takes a written accent to keep the stress in the correct place. In all other respects these verbs are regular. Note that **caer** (fall) and **oír** (hear) have a similar irregularity, but are also irregular in other ways.

IMPERATIVE

(tú) lee
(usted) lea
(vosotros) leed
(ustedes) lean

FUTURE
leeré

FUTURE PERFECT
habré leído

CONDITIONAL
leería

CONDITIONAL PERFECT
habría/hubiera leído

PRESENT SUBJUNCTIVE
lea
leas
lea
leamos
leáis
lean

PERFECT SUBJUNCTIVE
haya leído

IMPERFECT SUBJUNCTIVE
leyera/leyese

PLUPERFECT SUBJUNCTIVE
hubiera/hubiese leído

Léelo **en voz alta.**	*Read* it aloud.
No ***oyeron*** **nada.**	*They heard* nothing.
Leyó **el periódico de cabo a rabo.**	*He read* the newspaper from cover to cover.

14 enviar send

verbs with stressed weak vowel: **i → í**

GERUND	***PAST PARTICIPLE***
enviando	enviado

PRESENT
envío
envías
envía
enviamos
enviáis
envían

PERFECT
he enviado

PRESENT PROGRESSIVE
estoy enviando

IMPERFECT PROGRESSIVE
estaba enviando

IMPERFECT
enviaba

PRETERITE
envié

PLUPERFECT
había enviado

PAST ANTERIOR
hube enviado

Similar verbs

confiar	confide, entrust	**fiar**	trust
criar	rear, bring up	**guiar**	guide
desafiar	challenge, defy	**liar**	bind, tie
desviar	divert	**vaciar**	empty

Notes These (but not all) **-iar** verbs require an accent on the **-i-** when it is stressed, as shown above. The endings are all regular.

IMPERATIVE

(tú) envía
(usted) envíe
(vosotros) enviad
(ustedes) envíen

FUTURE

enviaré

FUTURE PERFECT

habré enviado

CONDITIONAL

enviaría

CONDITIONAL PERFECT

habría/hubiera enviado

PRESENT SUBJUNCTIVE

envíe
envíes
envíe
enviemos
enviéis
envíen

PERFECT SUBJUNCTIVE

haya enviado

IMPERFECT SUBJUNCTIVE

enviara/enviase

PLUPERFECT SUBJUNCTIVE

hubiera/hubiese enviado

Me fío **de ti, hijo.**	*I'm relying* on you, son.
Pepe *criaba* ovejas en Alcalá.	Pepe *used to raise* sheep in Alcalá.
Vacíen **ustedes sus bolsillos.**	*Empty* your pockets.
Mi amigo me *confió* un secreto.	My friend *told* me a secret.

verbs with stressed weak vowel: **u → ú**

GERUND	***PAST PARTICIPLE***
actuando	actuado

PRESENT
actúo
actúas
actúa
actuamos
actuáis
actúan

PERFECT
he actuado

PRESENT PROGRESSIVE
estoy actuando

IMPERFECT PROGRESSIVE
estaba actuando

IMPERFECT
actuaba

PRETERITE
actué

PLUPERFECT
había actuado

PAST ANTERIOR
hube actuado

Similar verbs

continuar	continue	**exceptuar**	except
devaluar	devalue	**insinuar**	insinuate
evaluar	evaluate	**perpetuar**	perpetuate

Notes The accent is needed on certain forms to keep the stress in the correct place. The endings are regular. Note also that some verbs require an accent on the **-i-** of the stem when it is stressed **aislar** (isolate) and **prohibir** (prohibit) and **reunir(se)** (join) needs an accent on the **-u-** when it is stressed.

IMPERATIVE

(tú) actúa
(usted) actúe
(vosotros) actuad
(ustedes) actúen

FUTURE

actuaré

FUTURE PERFECT

habré actuado

CONDITIONAL

actuaría

CONDITIONAL PERFECT

habría/hubiera actuado

PRESENT SUBJUNCTIVE

actúe
actúes
actúe
actuemos
actuéis
actúen

PERFECT SUBJUNCTIVE

haya actuado

IMPERFECT SUBJUNCTIVE

actuara/actuase

PLUPERFECT SUBJUNCTIVE

hubiera/hubiese actuado

El arbitro *actuó* bien en ese partido.	The referee *conducted* the match well.
Mi padre *actúa* de profesor a mi hermano.	My father *is acting* as my brother's teacher.

verbs whose stem ends in **-ll-**

GERUND	***PAST PARTICIPLE***
zambullendo	zambullido

PRESENT
zambullo

PERFECT
he zambullido

PRESENT PROGRESSIVE
estoy zambullendo

IMPERFECT PROGRESSIVE
estaba zambullendo

IMPERFECT
zambullía

PRETERITE
zambullí
zambulliste
zambulló
zambullimos
zambullisteis
zambulleron

PLUPERFECT
había zambullido

PAST ANTERIOR
hube zambullido

Similar verbs

engullir	gobble, gulp	**escabullirse**	slip away

Notes Due to the **-ll-**, the **-i-** disappears in certain forms, as shown in the lists above, when followed by another – stressed – vowel.

IMPERATIVE

(tú) zambulle
(usted) zambulla
(vosotros) zambullid
(ustedes) zambullan

FUTURE
zambulliré

FUTURE PERFECT
habré zambullido

CONDITIONAL
zambulliría

CONDITIONAL PERFECT
habría/hubiera zambullido

PRESENT SUBJUNCTIVE
zambulla

PERFECT SUBJUNCTIVE
haya zambullido

IMPERFECT SUBJUNCTIVE
zambullera/zambullese
zambulleras/zambulleses
zambullera/zambullese
zambulléramos/zambullésemos
zambullerais/zambulleseis
zambulleran/zambullesen

PLUPERFECT SUBJUNCTIVE
hubiera/hubiese zambullido

El ladrón *se escabulló* con las joyas.	The thief *got away* with the jewels.
Están *zambulléndose* en el agua.	They're *diving* into the water.
¡No *engullas* tu manzana!	Don't *gobble* your apple!

verbs whose stem ends in **-ñ-**

GERUND	PAST PARTICIPLE
gruñendo	gruñido

PRESENT
gruño

PRESENT PROGRESSIVE
estoy gruñendo

IMPERFECT
gruñía

PLUPERFECT
había gruñido

PERFECT
he gruñido

IMPERFECT PROGRESSIVE
estaba gruñendo

PRETERITE
gruñí
gruñiste
gruñó
gruñimos
gruñisteis
gruñeron

PAST ANTERIOR
hube gruñido

Similar verbs

ceñir	gird, surround, skirt	**tañer**	play, pluck *(instrument)*
reñir	scold, quarrel	**teñir**	dye

Notes Due to the **-ñ-**, the **-i-** disappears in certain forms, as shown in the lists above, when followed by another – stressed – vowel.

IMPERATIVE
(tú) gruñe
(usted) gruña
(vosotros) gruñid
(ustedes) gruñan

FUTURE
gruñiré

FUTURE PERFECT
habré gruñido

CONDITIONAL
gruñiría

CONDITIONAL PERFECT
habría/hubiera gruñido

PRESENT SUBJUNCTIVE
gruña

PERFECT SUBJUNCTIVE
haya gruñido

IMPERFECT SUBJUNCTIVE
gruñera/gruñese
gruñeras/gruñeses
gruñera/gruñese
gruñéramos/gruñésemos
gruñerais/gruñeseis
gruñeran/gruñesen

PLUPERFECT SUBJUNCTIVE
hubiera/hubiese gruñido

¡No me *riñas* así!	Don't *tell* me *off* like that!
La profesora *riñó* a las chicas.	The teacher *scolded* the girls.
Los músicos *tañeron* suavemente.	The musicians *played* softly.

forms with a **-g-**

GERUND
asiendo

PAST PARTICIPLE
asido

PRESENT
asgo
ases
ase
asimos
asís
asen

PERFECT
he asido

PRESENT PROGRESSIVE
estoy asiendo

IMPERFECT PROGRESSIVE
estaba asiendo

IMPERFECT
asía

PRETERITE
así

PLUPERFECT
había asido

PAST ANTERIOR
hube asido

Note In practice, the forms containing a **-g-** are avoided by using a different verb.

IMPERATIVE

(tú) ase	(vosotros) asid
(usted) asga	(ustedes) asgan

FUTURE
asiré

FUTURE PERFECT
habré asido

CONDITIONAL
asiría

CONDITIONAL PERFECT
habría/hubiera asido

PRESENT SUBJUNCTIVE
asga
asgas
asga
asgamos
asgáis
asgan

PERFECT SUBJUNCTIVE
haya asido

IMPERFECT SUBJUNCTIVE
asiera/asiese

PLUPERFECT SUBJUNCTIVE
hubiera/hubiese asido

Me *así* a la barra para no caer.	I *grabbed* the bar so as not to fall.
¡*Asgate* a esa rama!	*Grab* that branch!
Siempre me *asgo* a algo.	I always *hold* onto something.

19 pensar think

type 1 stem-changing verb **e → ie**

GERUND
pensando

PAST PARTICIPLE
pensado

PRESENT
pienso
piensas
piensa
pensamos
pensáis
piensan

PERFECT
he pensado

PRESENT PROGRESSIVE
estoy pensando

IMPERFECT PROGRESSIVE
estaba pensando

IMPERFECT
pensaba

PRETERITE
pensé
pensaste
pensó
pensamos
pensasteis
pensaron

Similar verbs

cerrar	close	**encender**	light, switch on
comenzar	commence	**entender**	understand
empezar	begin	**sentar(se)**	sit down

(This is only a very small selection of **e → ie** stem-changing verbs.)

Notes These verbs are type 1 stem-changing verbs. They are irregular only in the present indicative and present subjunctive, and therefore in the imperative forms except for the **vosotros** form (**pensad**). What happens is that the **-e-** in the stem changes to **-ie-** in those forms in which the stress falls on the syllable containing the **-e-**. In the forms which have the stress on the ending, the **-e-** remains. Since it is only in the present indicative and present subjunctive where some forms have the stress on the stem, this change does not occur in the other tenses. Note that some are **-ar** verbs and some are **-er** verbs and have the regular endings for their group. Verbs ending in **-zar** and **-gar** are also spelling-change verbs: ➤*Model verbs* 6 and 7 respectively.

IMPERATIVE
(tú) piensa
(usted) piense
(vosotros) pensad
(ustedes) piensen

PLUPERFECT
había pensado

PAST ANTERIOR
hube pensado

FUTURE
pensaré

FUTURE PERFECT
habré pensado

CONDITIONAL
pensaría

CONDITIONAL PERFECT
habría/hubiera pensado

PRESENT SUBJUNCTIVE
piense
pienses
piense
pensemos
penséis
piensen

PERFECT SUBJUNCTIVE
haya pensado

IMPERFECT SUBJUNCTIVE
pensara/pensase

PLUPERFECT SUBJUNCTIVE
hubiera/hubiese pensado

La receta
Conque, ¿hace frío? ¿*Nieva*? Pues lo que necesitas es un buen plato de sopa de patatas. Te la *recomendamos*. Preparación: ¡primero, recoge las patatas que *sembraste* en la primavera! Pélalas, y *hiérvelas* en agua durante diez minutos. Sácalas del agua, pásalas por la licuadora y añade un poco de agua. *Caliéntalo* bien, y ¡ya tienes tu sopa de patatas! *Siéntate*, *despliega* tu servilleta y *empieza* a comer. Será tan rica que comerás demasiado . . . *revientas* de sopa de patatas. Y después, ¡*friega* bien los platos!

The recipe
So, it's cold? *It's snowing?* Well, what you need is a nice bowl of potato soup. *We recommend* it. Preparation: first, dig up the potatoes *you planted* in the spring! Peel them and *boil them* in water for ten minutes. Take them out of the water, put them through the food processor and add some water. *Heat it up* well, and there you have your potato soup. *Sit down*, *unfold* your napkin and *start* to eat. It will be so delicious that you will eat too much . . . *you are bursting* with potato soup. Afterwards, *wash* the plates well!

20 volver return

type 1 stem-changing verb **o → ue**

GERUND	***PAST PARTICIPLE***
volviendo	vuelto

PRESENT
vuelvo
vuelves
vuelve
volvemos
volvéis
vuelven

PERFECT
he vuelto

PRESENT PROGRESSIVE
estoy volviendo

IMPERFECT PROGRESSIVE
estaba volviendo

IMPERFECT
volvía

PRETERITE
volví

PLUPERFECT
había vuelto

PAST ANTERIOR
hube vuelto

Similar verbs

acordarse	remember	**encontrar**	find; meet
costar	cost	**soler**	be accustomed/used to

(These are only four of the many **o → ue** stem-changing verbs.)

Notes These verbs are type 1 stem-changing verbs and are irregular only in the present indicative and present subjunctive, and thus also in the imperative forms except the **vosotros** form (**volved**). The **-o-** in the stem changes to **-ue-** in forms where the stress falls on the syllable containing the **-o-**. In forms which have the stress on the ending, the **-o-** remains. Since it is only in the present and present subjunctive where some forms have the stress on the stem, this change does not occur in the other tenses. Most of these are in other respects regular, but note, for example, the irregular past participle of **volver** (**vuelto**) and also of its compound forms, such as **envolver** (**envuelto**) and **resolver** (**resuelto**). All of these verbs are either **-ar** or **-er** verbs and take the regular endings for their group. Note, however, that verbs ending in **-car**, **-zar** or **-gar** are also spelling-change verbs: ➤*Model verbs* 5, 6 and 7 respectively.

IMPERATIVE

(tú) vuelve
(usted) vuelva

(vosotros) volved
(ustedes) vuelvan

FUTURE

volveré

FUTURE PERFECT

habré vuelto

CONDITIONAL

volvería

CONDITIONAL PERFECT

habría/hubiera vuelto

PRESENT SUBJUNCTIVE

vuelva
vuelvas
vuelva
volvamos
volváis
vuelvan

PERFECT SUBJUNCTIVE

haya vuelto

IMPERFECT SUBJUNCTIVE

volviera/volviese

PLUPERFECT SUBJUNCTIVE

hubiera/hubiese vuelto

La pesadilla

Normalmente *me acuesto* a medianoche, y *suelo* dormir bien . . . Pero ya son las ocho . . . Me levanto, *tuesto* un trozo de pan, y lo olvido. Mi mujer me *muestra* la carta que ha recibido . . . y de pronto *recuerdo* el pan. ¡Cómo *huele* el pan quemado! Voy a llegar tarde al trabajo, así que salgo corriendo. *Llueve* a cántaros: cojo el coche y al final de la calle *vuelca* al doblar la esquina. *Vuelvo* a casa a pie, y ¡me *muerde* un perro! ¡Cómo me *duele* la pierna! Luego de repente *me despierto* . . . Estaba *soñando*, nada más, y ¡*me duele* la pierna porque he caído de la cama!

The nightmare

Normally *I go to bed* at midnight, and I *usually* sleep well . . . But it's already eight o'clock . . . I get up, *toast* a piece of bread, and I forget it. My wife *shows* me the letter she has received . . . and *I* suddenly *remember* the bread. Doesn't burned bread *smell* bad! I'm going to be late for work, so I run out. *It's raining* heavily: I set off in the car, and at the end of the street *it turns over* going around the corner. I *go home* on foot and a dog bites me! My leg really *hurts*! Then suddenly *I wake up* . . . I was just *dreaming*, and my leg hurts because I've fallen out of bed!

21 jugar — play

type 1 stem-changing verb **u → ue**

GERUND
jugando

PAST PARTICIPLE
jugado

PRESENT
juego
juegas
juega
jugamos
jugáis
juegan

PERFECT
he jugado

PRESENT PROGRESSIVE
estoy jugando

IMPERFECT PROGRESSIVE
estaba jugando

IMPERFECT
jugaba
jugabas
jugaba
jugábamos
jugábais
jugaban

PRETERITE
jugué
jugaste
jugó
jugamos
jugasteis
jugaron

Notes **Jugar** is unique in having the **u → ue** spelling change, so there are no other similar verbs. To all intents and purposes, it is a member of the type 1 **o → ue** family. These verbs are irregular only in the present indicative and present subjunctive, and therefore in the imperative forms except for the **vosotros** form (**jugad**).

What happens with **jugar** is that the **-u-** in the stem changes to **-ue-** in those forms in which the stress falls on the syllable containing **-u-**. In those forms which have the stress on the ending, the **-u-** remains. Since it is only in the present and present subjunctive where some forms have the stress on the stem, this change does not occur in the other tenses.

Note, however, the **u** in the first person singular of the preterite tense and in the whole of the present subjunctive. This is simply to preserve the pronunciation of the hard **g** in those forms where the verb ending begins with an **e**.

IMPERATIVE
(tú) juega
(usted) juegue
(vosotros) jugad
(ustedes) jueguen

PLUPERFECT
había jugado

PAST ANTERIOR
hube jugado

FUTURE
jugaré

FUTURE PERFECT
habré jugado

CONDITIONAL
jugaría

CONDITIONAL PERFECT
habría/hubiera jugado

PRESENT SUBJUNCTIVE
juegue
juegues
juegue
juguemos
juguéis
jueguen

PERFECT SUBJUNCTIVE
haya jugado

IMPERFECT SUBJUNCTIVE
jugara/jugase

PLUPERFECT SUBJUNCTIVE
hubiera/hubiese jugado

Los jugadores	**The players**
MARADONA *JUEGA* OTRA VEZ CON LA SELECCIÓN ARGENTINA	MARADONA *PLAYS* FOR ARGENTINA AGAIN
EL ATLETIC DE BILBAO *JUGARÁ* MAÑANA EN EL ESTADIO BERNABEU	ATLETIC DE BILBAO *WILL PLAY* TOMORROW AT THE BERNABEU STADIUM
ARANTCHA SANCHEZ VICARIO NO *JUGÓ* EN WIMBLEDON A CAUSA DE SU ENFERMEDAD	ARANTCHA SANCHEZ VICARIO DID NOT *PLAY* AT WIMBLEDON DUE TO HER ILLNESS
"*JUGUÉ* MUY MAL EN ST ANDREWS" CONFIESA SEVE BALLESTEROS	*I PLAYED* BADLY AT ST ANDREWS, SEVE BALLESTEROS CONFESSES
"LOS NIÑOS QUE *JUEGAN* EN LA CALLE CORREN GRANDES RIESGOS" AFIRMA EL DIRECTOR GENERAL DE SANIDAD	CHILDREN WHO *PLAY* IN THE STREET RUN GREAT RISKS, SAYS THE DIRECTOR OF PUBLIC HEALTH

type 2 stem-changing verb **e → ie** and **i**

GERUND	***PAST PARTICIPLE***
sintiendo	sentido

PRESENT
siento
sientes
siente
sentimos
sentís
sienten

PERFECT
he sentido

PRESENT PROGRESSIVE
estoy sintiendo

IMPERFECT PROGRESSIVE
estaba sintiendo

IMPERFECT
sentía

PRETERITE
sentí
sentiste
sintió
sentimos
sentisteis
sintieron

Similar verbs

advertir	warn, advise	**mentir**	lie
diferir	differ	**preferir**	prefer
divertirse	enjoy oneself	**referir**	refer, relate
herir	wound	**sugerir**	suggest

(These are among the most common stem-changing verbs of this type.)

Notes These verbs are type 2 stem-changing verbs and are all **-ir** verbs. They have the change **e → ie** in some forms of the present indicative and present subjunctive, and therefore also in the imperative forms except the **vosotros** form (**sentid**). What happens is that the **-e-** in the stem changes to **-ie-** in those forms in which the stress falls on the syllable containing the **-e-**. In those forms which have the stress on the ending, the **-e-** remains. In addition, these verbs have a change from **e → i** in the gerund, in the first and second persons plural of the present, in the third person forms of the preterite, and in all forms of the imperfect subjunctive. These verbs are regular in other respects.

IMPERATIVE
(tú) siente
(usted) sienta
(vosotros) sentid
(ustedes) sientan

PLUPERFECT
había sentido

PAST ANTERIOR
hube sentido

FUTURE
sentiré

FUTURE PERFECT
habré sentido

CONDITIONAL
sentiría

CONDITIONAL PERFECT
habría/hubiera sentido

PRESENT SUBJUNCTIVE
sienta
sientas
sienta
sintamos
sintáis
sientan

PERFECT SUBJUNCTIVE
haya sentido

IMPERFECT SUBJUNCTIVE
sintiera/sintiese

PLUPERFECT SUBJUNCTIVE
hubiera/hubiese sentido

La Reconquista
En tiempos de la Reconquista, había mucha intolerancia religiosa. Muchos musulmanes *se convirtieron* a cristianos y viceversa. Otros no lo hicieron, y si no se *arrepentían*, *sintieron* toda la ira de sus enemigos. Algunos *mentían* para escaparse.
La Mili
En España, todos los jóvenes tienen que hacer la Mili: los españoles usan esta palabra cuando *se refieren* al servicio militar obligatorio. Algunos *se divierten* mucho pero otros muchos *prefieren* no hacerlo.

The Reconquest
In the times of the Reconquest there was a lot of religious intolerance. Many Muslims *became* Christians and vice versa. Others did not do so, and if *they* did not *repent*, *they felt* the full wrath of their enemies. Some *lied* in order to escape.
Military service
In Spain, all young men have to do "la Mili": the Spanish use this term to *refer* to compulsory military service. Some really *enjoy* it, but many others *prefer* not to do it.

type 2 stem-changing verb **o → ue** and **u**

GERUND	*PAST PARTICIPLE*
durmiendo	dormido

PRESENT
duermo
duermes
duerme
dormimos
dormís
duermen

PERFECT
he dormido

PRESENT PROGRESSIVE
estoy durmiendo

IMPERFECT PROGRESSIVE
estaba durmiendo

IMPERFECT
dormía

PRETERITE
dormí
dormiste
durmió
dormimos
dormisteis
durmieron

Similar verb

morir die

Notes These verbs are type 2 stem-changing verbs. They change from **o → ue** in the present indicative and present subjunctive, and therefore also in the imperative forms except the **vosotros** form (**dormid**). What happens is that the **-o-** in the stem changes to **-ue-** in those forms in which the stress falls on the syllable containing the **-o-**. In those forms which have the stress on the ending, the **-o-** remains. In addition, these two verbs change from **o → u** in the gerund, in the third person forms of the preterite, in all forms of the imperfect subjunctive, and in the first and second persons plural of the present subjunctive. All of these have an ending beginning with an **-i-**. These verbs are regular in other respects, but note the irregular past participle of **morir** (**muerto**).

IMPERATIVE

(tú) duerme
(usted) duerma
(vosotros) dormid
(ustedes) duerman

PLUPERFECT

había dormido

PAST ANTERIOR

hube dormido

FUTURE

dormiré

FUTURE PERFECT

habré dormido

CONDITIONAL

dormiría

CONDITIONAL PERFECT

habría/hubiera dormido

PRESENT SUBJUNCTIVE

duerma
duermas
duerma
durmamos
durmáis
duerman

PERFECT SUBJUNCTIVE

haya dormido

IMPERFECT SUBJUNCTIVE

durmiera/durmiese

PLUPERFECT SUBJUNCTIVE

hubiera/hubiese dormido

Unos titulares

MUEREN **CINCO PERSONAS EN UN ACCIDENTE DE TRÁFICO**

SIDA: UN MILLÓN DE VÍCTIMAS *MORIRÁN* ESTE AÑO

MURIÓ **ENRIQUE TIERNO GALVAN: EL ALCALDE MÁS POPULAR QUE JAMÁS TUVO MADRID**

SE DURMIÓ **AL VOLANTE DE SU NUEVO MERCEDES . . .**

Some headlines

FIVE PEOPLE *DIE* IN A TRAFFIC ACCIDENT

AIDS: A MILLION VICTIMS *WILL DIE* THIS YEAR

ENRIQUE TIERNO GALVAN *DIES*: THE MOST POPULAR MAYOR MADRID HAS EVER HAD

HE FELL ASLEEP AT THE WHEEL OF OF HIS NEW MERCEDES . . .

Un poco de publicidad

¡*DUERMA* BIEN CON UN COLCHÓN FLEX!

¡150 KILÓMETROS POR HORA MIENTRAS *DUERME* . . . Y LLEVE SU COCHE! . . . EN AUTO-EXPRESO

A few advertisements

SLEEP WELL WITH A FLEX MATTRESS!

150 KILOMETERS PER HOUR WHILE *YOU SLEEP* . . . AND TAKE YOUR CAR! . . . BY MOTORAIL

type 3 stem-changing verb **e → i**

GERUND	***PAST PARTICIPLE***
pidiendo	pedido

PRESENT
pido
pides
pide
pedimos
pedís
piden

PERFECT
he pedido

PRESENT PROGRESSIVE
estoy pidiendo

IMPERFECT PROGRESSIVE
estaba pidiendo

IMPERFECT
pedía

PRETERITE
pedí
pediste
pidió
pedimos
pedisteis
pidieron

Similar verbs

conseguir	manage, get hold of	**reñir**	scold
corregir	correct	**repetir**	repeat
despedir	say goodbye, fire	**seguir**	follow, carry on
elegir	elect, choose	**servir**	serve
gemir	groan	**sonreír**	smile
impedir	prevent	**teñir**	dye
regir	rule	**vestirse**	dress
reírse	laugh		

(plus any compounds of these verbs)

Notes These verbs, which are all **-ir** verbs, are type 3 spelling-change verbs. They have the spelling change **e → i** in most forms of the present indicative and all of the present subjunctive, and therefore in the imperative forms except for the **vosotros** form (**pedid**). It also occurs in the third person forms of the preterite and in all forms of the imperfect subjunctive forms, and in the gerund.

IMPERATIVE
(tú) pide
(usted) pida
(vosotros) pedid
(ustedes) pidan

PLUPERFECT
había pedido

PAST ANTERIOR
hube pedido

FUTURE
pediré

FUTURE PERFECT
habré pedido

CONDITIONAL
pediría

CONDITIONAL PERFECT
habría/hubiera pedido

PRESENT SUBJUNCTIVE
pida
pidas
pida
pidamos
pidáis
pidan

PERFECT SUBJUNCTIVE
haya pedido

IMPERFECT SUBJUNCTIVE
pidiera/pidiese

PLUPERFECT SUBJUNCTIVE
hubiera/hubiese pedido

Entrevista con el Presidente	**Interview with the President**
– Bueno, señor, unas preguntas: primero, ¿por qué *se viste* así?	– Well, Sir, a few questions: first, why *do you dress* like that?
– Pues, porque *sirvo* a mi país como soldado. Cuando me *eligieron*, ya era general, por lo tanto *sigo* con el uniforme.	– Well, because *I serve* my country as a soldier. When *they elected* me, I was already a general, so *I have kept* the uniform.
– ¿Por qué *sonríe* tanto?	– Why *are you smiling* so much?
– Porque cuando era niño mi madre me *reñía* tanto que mis amigos *se reían* de mí. Y ahora soy jefe de todos. Ninguno *consiguió* lo que yo he *conseguido*.	– Because when I was a child, my mother *scolded* me so much that my friends *used to laugh* at me. And now I am their boss. None of them *has achieved* what I *have*.
– ¿Hasta cuándo será Presidente?	– Until when will you be President?
– ¡Hasta cuando me *despidan*!	– Until *they fire* me!

Irregular verbs

The following are the most common irregular verbs in Spanish. Some are included only because they have a unique spelling change, or because they do not conform to a predictable pattern.

In the future and conditional, only the stem can be irregular – the same set of endings is always used. Therefore, only the first person singular form is given. For the full set of endings, see *The complete system of tenses in Spanish* [➤*Model verb 1*]. Any irregularity in the future tense stem will apply to the conditional.

Except for **ser** and **ir**, the imperfect tense of all verbs is regular, and either the **-ar** or **-er/-ir** set of endings is used. Therefore, only the first person singular form is given, since the others are easy to work out from the *Regular verbs* [➤*Model verbs* 2,3,4].

Similarly, compound tenses using **estar** or **haber** are not given in full: simply consult the tables for **estar** or **haber** [➤*Model verbs 38,40*] or look at *The complete system of tenses in Spanish* [➤*Model verb 1*].

Verbs with a **pretérito grave** [➤*The verb system in Spanish* 10b(ix)] are marked (**pg**).

Verbs with a present indicative and subjunctive which follow the stem-change pattern described in *The verb system in Spanish* 10b(v) [➤*Model verbs19-24*] are marked (**sc**).

25 abrir open

GERUND	*PAST PARTICIPLE*
abriendo	abierto

PRESENT	*PERFECT*
abro	he abierto
abres	
abre	
abrimos	
abrís	
abren	

PRESENT PROGRESSIVE	*IMPERFECT PROGRESSIVE*
estoy abriendo	estaba abriendo

IMPERFECT	*PRETERITE*
abría	abrí
abrías	abriste
abría	abrió
abríamos	abrimos
abríais	abristeis
abrían	abrieron

Similar verbs

cubrir	cover	**entreabrir**	half open
descubrir	uncover		

Notes The only irregularity lies in the formation of the past participle. In every other respect, this is a regular verb of the **-ir** family.

IMPERATIVE
(tú) abre
(usted) abra
(vosotros) abrid
(ustedes) abran

PLUPERFECT
había abierto

PAST ANTERIOR
hube abierto

FUTURE
abriré

FUTURE PERFECT
habré abierto

CONDITIONAL
abriría

CONDITIONAL PERFECT
habría/hubiera abierto

PRESENT SUBJUNCTIVE
abra
abras
abra
abramos
abráis
abran

PERFECT SUBJUNCTIVE
haya abierto

IMPERFECT SUBJUNCTIVE
abriera/abriese

PLUPERFECT SUBJUNCTIVE
hubiera/hubiese abierto

Unos avisos	**A few notices**
ABIERTO **DE 9 A 10**	*OPEN* FROM 9 TO 10
ESTAS PUERTAS QUEDAN *ABIERTAS* DÍA Y NOCHE	THESE GATES REMAIN *OPEN* DAY AND NIGHT
ABRA **EL GRIFO/LA PAJA CON CUIDADO**	*TURN* THE FAUCET/TAP *ON* WITH CARE
ESTA PUERTA *SE ABRE* CON CARTA ELECTRÓNICA SOLAMENTE	THIS DOOR *OPENS* WITH AN ELECTRONIC CARD ONLY
ABRIMOS **EL 1° DE SEPTIEMBRE**	*WE OPEN* ON SEPTEMBER 1ST

(sc)

GERUND
adquiriendo

PAST PARTICIPLE
adquirido

PRESENT
adquiero
adquieres
adquiere
adquirimos
adquirís
adquieren

PERFECT
he adquirido

PRESENT PROGRESSIVE
estoy adquiriendo

IMPERFECT PROGRESSIVE
estaba adquiriendo

IMPERFECT
adquiría

PRETERITE
adquirí
adquiriste
adquirió
adquirimos
adquiristeis
adquirieron

Notes This verb is largely like **querer** and as such behaves like a stem-changing verb when the stem vowel is stressed; elsewhere, the **-i-** of the infinitive stem remains.

IMPERATIVE

(tú) adquiere
(usted) adquiera
(vosotros) adquirid
(ustedes) adquieran

PLUPERFECT

había adquirido

PAST ANTERIOR

hube adquirido

FUTURE

adquiriré

FUTURE PERFECT

habré adquirido

CONDITIONAL

adquiriría

CONDITIONAL PERFECT

habría/hubiera adquirido

PRESENT SUBJUNCTIVE

adquiera
adquieras
adquiera
adquiramos
adquiráis
adquieran

PERFECT SUBJUNCTIVE

haya adquirido

IMPERFECT SUBJUNCTIVE

adquiriera/adquiriese

PLUPERFECT SUBJUNCTIVE

hubiera/hubiese adquirido

Tengo que *adquirir* un empleo muy pronto. — I need to *get* a job very soon.

***Adquirimos* un canguro muy bueno** — We *found* a good babysitter.

(pg)

GERUND	***PAST PARTICIPLE***
andando	andado

PRESENT
ando
andas
anda
andamos
andáis
andan

PERFECT
he andado

PRESENT PROGRESSIVE
estoy andando

IMPERFECT PROGRESSIVE
estaba andando

IMPERFECT
andaba

PRETERITE
anduve
anduviste
anduvo
anduvimos
anduvisteis
anduvieron

Notes The preterite, and consequently the imperfect subjunctive (of **pretérito grave** type) is the only irregularity. In every other respect, **andar** behaves like a regular **-ar** verb.

IMPERATIVE	
(tú) anda	(vosotros) andad
(usted) ande	(ustedes) anden

PLUPERFECT	***PAST ANTERIOR***
había andado	hube andado
FUTURE	***FUTURE PERFECT***
andaré	habré andado
CONDITIONAL	***CONDITIONAL PERFECT***
andaría	habría/hubiera andado
PRESENT SUBJUNCTIVE	***PERFECT SUBJUNCTIVE***
ande andes ande andemos andéis anden	haya andado
IMPERFECT SUBJUNCTIVE	***PLUPERFECT SUBJUNCTIVE***
anduviera/anduviese	hubiera/hubiese andado

¡*Anda*!	*Come on! Get away!*
Dime con quien *andas* y te diré quién eres.	Tell me who *you go around* with and I'll tell you who you are. (proverb)
Mi coche no *anda*.	My car *is* not working.
Fuimos *andando* a la sierra.	We *walked* to the mountains.
¿Qué tal *andas*?	How *are you getting on*?

(sc + pg)

GERUND	***PAST PARTICIPLE***
bendiciendo	bendecido

PRESENT
bendigo
bendices
bendice
bendecimos
bendecís
bendicen

PERFECT
he bendecido

PRESENT PROGRESSIVE
estoy bendiciendo

IMPERFECT PROGRESSIVE
estaba bendiciendo

IMPERFECT
bendecía
bendecías
bendecía
bendecíamos
bendecíais
bendecían

PRETERITE
bendije
bendijiste
bendijo
bendijimos
bendijisteis
bendijeron

PLUPERFECT
había bendecido

PAST ANTERIOR
hube bendecido

Similar verb

maldecir curse

Notes The key irregularities are:

- the first person singular of the present tense, and therefore all of the present subjunctive with **-g-** in place of **-c-**;
- the present indicative, which behaves like a type 3 stem-changing verb;
- the **pretérito grave** and therefore the imperfect subjunctive.

In other respects, **bendecir** is like a regular **-ir** verb. It largely follows its 'parent' verb, **decir**, but with the following exceptions:

- the past participle, which is regular, unlike **decir** (**dicho**);
- the singular familiar imperative **bendice** (unlike **di**);
- the regular formation of the future and conditional stem.

IMPERATIVE

(tú) bendice
(usted) bendiga
(vosotros) bendecid
(ustedes) bendigan

FUTURE

bendeciré
bendecirás
bendecirá
bendeciremos
bendeciréis
bendecirán

FUTURE PERFECT

habré bendecido

CONDITIONAL

bendeciría

CONDITIONAL PERFECT

habría/hubiera bendecido

PRESENT SUBJUNCTIVE

bendiga
bendigas
bendiga
bendigamos
bendigáis
bendigan

PERFECT SUBJUNCTIVE

haya bendecido

IMPERFECT SUBJUNCTIVE

bendijera/bendijese

PLUPERFECT SUBJUNCTIVE

hubiera/hubiese bendecido

¡*Bendígame* Padre, pues he pecado! — *Bless me* Father, for I have sinned!

¡Dios te *bendiga*! — May God *bless* you!

(pg)

GERUND
cabiendo

PAST PARTICIPLE
cabido

PRESENT
quepo
cabes
cabe
cabemos
cabéis
caben

PERFECT
he cabido

PRESENT PROGRESSIVE
estoy cabiendo

IMPERFECT PROGRESSIVE
estaba cabiendo

IMPERFECT
cabía

PRETERITE
cupe
cupiste
cupo
cupimos
cupisteis
cupieron

Notes The key irregularities are:

- the first person singular of the present tense, and present subjunctive;
- the **pretérito grave** and therefore the imperfect subjunctive;
- the future tense stem.

IMPERATIVE

(tú) cabe
(usted) quepa
(vosotros) cabed
(ustedes) quepan

PLUPERFECT
había cabido

PAST ANTERIOR
hube cabido

FUTURE
cabré

FUTURE PERFECT
habré cabido

CONDITIONAL
cabría

CONDITIONAL PERFECT
habría/hubiera cabido

PRESENT SUBJUNCTIVE
quepa
quepas
quepa
quepamos
quepáis
quepan

PERFECT SUBJUNCTIVE
haya cabido

IMPERFECT SUBJUNCTIVE
cupiera/cupiese

PLUPERFECT SUBJUNCTIVE
hubiera/hubiese cabido

¡No *cabe* duda, no *cabemos* todos! — *There's* no doubt, *we* don't all *fit*!

GERUND	*PAST PARTICIPLE*
cayendo	caído

PRESENT	*PERFECT*
caigo	he caído
caes	
cae	
caemos	
caéis	
caen	

PRESENT PROGRESSIVE	*IMPERFECT PROGRESSIVE*
estoy cayendo	estaba cayendo

IMPERFECT	*PRETERITE*
caía	caí
	caíste
	cayó
	caímos
	caísteis
	cayeron

Similar verbs

decaer decay

Notes This verb displays a number of irregularities:

- the first person singular of the present indicative, and so all of the present subjunctive, is based on the stem **caig-**;
- a **-y-** is needed in the third person forms of the preterite;
- an accent is needed on the **-i-** where it is stressed.

The verbs **roer** (gnaw) and **corroer** (corrode) follow a largely similar pattern.

IMPERATIVE

(tú) cae
(usted) caiga
(vosotros) caed
(ustedes) caigan

PLUPERFECT
había caído

PAST ANTERIOR
hube caído

FUTURE
caeré

FUTURE PERFECT
habré caído

CONDITIONAL
caería

CONDITIONAL PERFECT
habría/hubiera caído

PRESENT SUBJUNCTIVE
cayera/cayese

PLUPERFECT SUBJUNCTIVE
hubiera/hubiese caído

¡Ten cuidado, o te *caerás*!	Be careful or *you will fall*!
***Se cayó* en un hoyo enorme.**	*He fell* into a large hole.
¡Lo dejé *caer*!	I *dropped* it!

(pg)

GERUND	***PAST PARTICIPLE***
conduciendo	conducido

PRESENT
conduzco
conduces
conduce
conducimos
conducís
conducen

PERFECT
he conducido

PRESENT PROGRESSIVE
estoy conduciendo

IMPERFECT PROGRESSIVE
estaba conduciendo

IMPERFECT
conducía

PRETERITE
conduje
condujiste
condujo
condujimos
condujisteis
condujeron

Similar verbs

All verbs ending in **-ducir**:

aducir	adduce	**producir**	produce
deducir	deduce	**reducir**	reduce
inducir	induce	**reproducir**	reproduce
introducir	introduce	**traducir**	translate

Notes The key irregularities are:

- the first person singular of the present tense, and therefore all of the present subjunctive with **-zc-** in place of **-c-**;
- the **pretérito grave** and therefore the imperfect subjunctive.

As can be seen, all are compounds of a base verb stem **-ducir**.

IMPERATIVE
(tú) conduce
(usted) conduzca
(vosotros) conducid
(ustedes) conduzcan

PLUPERFECT
había conducido

PAST ANTERIOR
hube conducido

FUTURE
conduciré

FUTURE PERFECT
habré conducido

CONDITIONAL
conduciría

CONDITIONAL PERFECT
habría/hubiera conducido

PRESENT SUBJUNCTIVE
conduzca
conduzcas
conduzca
conduzcamos
conduzcáis
conduzcan

PERFECT SUBJUNCTIVE
haya conducido

IMPERFECT SUBJUNCTIVE
condujera/condujese

PLUPERFECT SUBJUNCTIVE
hubiera/hubiese conducido

No sé *conducir*.	I don't know how to *drive*.
El profesor *tradujo* esta carta.	The teacher *translated* this letter.
***Introduzca* una moneda.**	*Put in* a coin.

GERUND	***PAST PARTICIPLE***
conociendo	conocido

PRESENT
conozco
conoces
conoce
conocemos
conocéis
conocen

PERFECT
he conocido

PRESENT PROGRESSIVE
estoy conociendo

IMPERFECT PROGRESSIVE
estaba conociendo

IMPERFECT
conocía

PRETERITE
conocí
conociste
conoció
conocimos
conocisteis
conocieron

Similar verbs

abastecer	provide, supply	**embellecer**	make beautiful
aborrecer	hate, abhor	**encanecer**	go gray
acontecer	happen	**endurecer (se)**	harden
agradecer	be grateful	**enfurecer**	get angry
amanecer	dawn	**enloquecer**	go mad
anochecer	get dark	**enriquecer (se)**	get rich
aparecer	appear	**ensordecer**	deafen
apetecer	feel like, fancy	**entristecer (se)**	sadden
carecer	lack	**envejecer**	grow old
compadecer	sympathize with	**envilecer**	degrade
crecer	grow	**esclarecer**	grow light
desaparecer	disappear	**establecer**	establish
desconocer	not know	**estremecerse**	shiver
desobedecer	disobey	**favorecer**	favor

IMPERATIVE

(tú) conoce
(usted) conozca
(vosotros) conoced
(ustedes) conozcan

PLUPERFECT
había conocido

PAST ANTERIOR
hube conocido

FUTURE
conoceré

FUTURE PERFECT
habré conocido

CONDITIONAL
conocería

CONDITIONAL PERFECT
habría/hubiera conocido

PRESENT SUBJUNCTIVE
conozca
conozcas
conozca
conozcamos
conozcáis
conozcan

PERFECT SUBJUNCTIVE
haya conocido

IMPERFECT SUBJUNCTIVE
conociera/conociese

PLUPERFECT SUBJUNCTIVE
hubiera/hubiese conocido

florecer	flower, bloom	**oscurecer**	grow dark
fortalecer	strengthen	**padecer**	suffer
humedecer	moisten	**palidecer**	grow pale
languidecer	languish	**parecer**	seem
merecer	deserve	**pertenecer**	belong
nacer	be born	**reconocer**	recognize

Notes The only irregularities are the first person singular of the present tense, and in consequence all forms of the present subjunctive.

***Nos conocimos* en Madrid.**	*We met* in Madrid.
Los niños *crecen* rápidamente.	Children *grow* quickly.
El autobús *desapareció* al final de la calle.	The bus *disappeared* at the end of the street.

GERUND
dando

PAST PARTICIPLE
dado

PRESENT
doy
das
da
damos
dais
dan

PERFECT
he dado

PRESENT PROGRESSIVE
estoy dando

IMPERFECT PROGRESSIVE
estaba dando

IMPERFECT
daba

PRETERITE
di
diste
dio
dimos
disteis
dieron

Notes The key irregularities are:

- the first person singular of the present tense, ending in **-oy**;
- the accent needed on the form **dé** to distinguish it from the preposition **de**;
- the preterite forms, in which **dar** behaves like an **-er/-ir** verb, and needs no written accents;
- the imperfect subjunctive, based on the preterite stem.

In all other respects, **dar** behaves like a regular **-ar** verb.

IMPERATIVE

(tú) da
(usted) dé
(vosotros) dad
(ustedes) den

PLUPERFECT
había dado

PAST ANTERIOR
hube dado

FUTURE
daré

FUTURE PERFECT
habré dado

CONDITIONAL
daría

CONDITIONAL PERFECT
habría/hubiera dado

PRESENT SUBJUNCTIVE
dé
des
dé
demos
deis
den

PERFECT SUBJUNCTIVE
haya dado

IMPERFECT SUBJUNCTIVE
diera/diese

PLUPERFECT SUBJUNCTIVE
hubiera/hubiese dado

***Déme* la sal, por favor.**	*Pass* the salt, please.
Mi padre sólo me *dio* cien pesetas.	My father *gave* me only a hundred pesetas.
Por el amor de Dios, ¡*dadme* una limosna!	For the love of God, *give* me alms!

34 decir — say, tell

(sc + pg)

GERUND	***PAST PARTICIPLE***
diciendo	dicho

PRESENT
digo
dices
dice
decimos
decís
dicen

PERFECT
he dicho

PRESENT PROGRESSIVE
estoy diciendo

IMPERFECT PROGRESSIVE
estaba diciendo

IMPERFECT
decía
decías
decía
decíamos
decíais
decían

PRETERITE
dije
dijiste
dijo
dijimos
dijisteis
dijeron

Similar verbs

contradecir	contradict	**predecir**	predict
desdecir(se)	clash with, withdraw		

Notes The key irregularities are:

- the first person singular of the present tense, and therefore all of the present subjunctive, with **-g-** in place of **-c-**;
- the present indicative, which behaves like a type 3 stem-changing verb;
- the **pretérito grave** and therefore the imperfect subjunctive;
- the past participle, similar to that of **hacer** (**hecho**);
- the future and conditional stem **dir-**.

In other respects, **decir** is like a regular **-ir** verb.

IMPERATIVE
(tú) di
(usted) diga
(vosotros) decid
(ustedes) digan

PLUPERFECT
había dicho

PAST ANTERIOR
hube dicho

FUTURE
diré

FUTURE PERFECT
habré dicho

CONDITIONAL
diría

CONDITIONAL PERFECT
habría/hubiera dicho

PRESENT SUBJUNCTIVE
diga
digas
diga
digamos
digáis
digan

PERFECT SUBJUNCTIVE
haya dicho

IMPERFECT SUBJUNCTIVE
dijera/dijese

PLUPERFECT SUBJUNCTIVE
hubiera/hubiese dicho

¡*Dicho* y hecho!	No sooner *said* than done!
***Diga*, por favor . . .**	Excuse me, can you *tell* me . . ?
¡*Dígame*!	*Hello! (on the telephone)*
¡*Dicen* que es loco!	*They say* he's crazy!
Me *dicen* que hace frío.	I'm *told* the weather's cold.
***Digan* lo que *digan* . . .**	Whatever they *say* . . .
. . . mejor *dicho* . . .	. . . that is to *say* . . .
¡Haberlo *dicho*!	You might have said!

GERUND
irguiendo

PAST PARTICIPLE
erguido

PRESENT
yergo/irgo
yergues/irgues
yergue/irgue
erguimos
erguís
yerguen/irguen

PERFECT
he erguido

PRESENT PROGRESSIVE
estoy irguiendo

IMPERFECT PROGRESSIVE
estaba irguiendo

IMPERFECT
erguía

PRETERITE
erguí
erguiste
irguió
erguimos
erguisteis
irguieron

Notes This verb has three possible stems, and as can be seen, in several forms two alternative forms exist. The **ye-** stem is basically due to this verb being a stem-changing verb: instead of beginning **ie-**, however, stressed-stem forms begin with **ye-**. Note the **-u-** needed in all forms in which the verb ending begins with an **-e**. The one regular feature is that all of the verb endings follow the pattern for a regular **-ir** verb [➤**vivir** *4*].

IMPERATIVE
(tú) yergue/irgue
(usted) yerga/irga
(vosotros) erguid
(ustedes) yergan/irgan

PLUPERFECT
había erguido

PAST ANTERIOR
hube erguido

FUTURE
erguiré

FUTURE PERFECT
habré erguido

CONDITIONAL
erguiría

CONDITIONAL PERFECT
habría/hubiera erguido

PRESENT SUBJUNCTIVE
yerga/irga
yergas/irgas
yerga/irga
yergamos/irgamos
yergáis/irgáis
yergan/irgan

PERFECT SUBJUNCTIVE
haya erguido

IMPERFECT SUBJUNCTIVE
irguiera/irguiese

PLUPERFECT SUBJUNCTIVE
hubiera/hubiese erguido

¡Ponte *erguido*!	*Straighten* up!
El enfermo *se irguió* en la cama.	The sick man *sat up* in bed.
Los caballos *irguieron* las orejas.	The horses *lifted/pricked* their ears.
La chica *erguía* la cabeza.	The girl *held* her head *up* high.

(sc)

GERUND
errando

PAST PARTICIPLE
errado

PRESENT
yerro
yerras
yerra
erramos
erráis
yerran

PERFECT
he errado

PRESENT PROGRESSIVE
estoy errando

IMPERFECT PROGRESSIVE
estaba errando

IMPERFECT
erraba

PRETERITE
erré
erraste
erró
erramos
errasteis
erraron

Notes This verb is basically a stem-changing **-ar** verb. However, rather than stressed-stem forms beginning **ie-**, they begin **ye-**. In forms where the stem is unstressed, the **err-** remains. All endings are those of a regular **-ar** verb.

IMPERATIVE

(tú) yerra
(usted) yerre
(vosotros) errad
(ustedes) yerren

PLUPERFECT
había errado

PAST ANTERIOR
hube errado

FUTURE
erraré

FUTURE PERFECT
habré errado

CONDITIONAL
erraría

CONDITIONAL PERFECT
habría/hubiera errado

PRESENT SUBJUNCTIVE
yerre
yerres
yerre
erremos
erréis
yerren

PERFECT SUBJUNCTIVE
haya errado

IMPERFECT SUBJUNCTIVE
errara/errase

PLUPERFECT SUBJUNCTIVE
hubiera/hubiese errado

El río *erraba* por el campo.	The river *wandered* through the countryside.
¡No *yerres* por ahí!	Don't *wander* through there!

GERUND	***PAST PARTICIPLE***
escribiendo	escrito

PRESENT
escribo
escribes
escribe
escribimos
escribís
escriben

PERFECT
he escrito

PRESENT PROGRESSIVE
estoy escribiendo

IMPERFECT PROGRESSIVE
estaba escribiendo

IMPERFECT
escribía
escribías
escribía
escribíamos
escribíais
escribían

PRETERITE
escribí
escribiste
escribió
escribimos
escribiste
escribieron

Similar verbs

describir	describe	**suscribir**	subscribe
inscribir	inscribe	**transcribir**	transcribe
proscribir	proscribe		

Notes Largely a regular **-ir** verb, but with an irregular past participle.

IMPERATIVE

(tú) escribe
(usted) escriba
(vosotros) escribid
(ustedes) escriban

PLUPERFECT
había escrito

PAST ANTERIOR
hube escrito

FUTURE
escribiré

FUTURE PERFECT
habré escrito

CONDITIONAL
escribiría

CONDITIONAL PERFECT
habría/hubiera escrito

PRESENT SUBJUNCTIVE
escriba
escribas
escriba
escribamos
escribáis
escriban

PERFECT SUBJUNCTIVE
haya escrito

IMPERFECT SUBJUNCTIVE
escribiera/escribiese

PLUPERFECT SUBJUNCTIVE
hubiera/hubiese escrito

¡*Escríbeme* pronto!	*Write* soon!
¡No *escribes* nada en tu pupitre!	Don't *write* anything on your desk!
Nuestros amigos nos han *escrito* de Méjico.	Our friends have *written* to us from Mexico.
José nos ha *descrito* a la chica.	José *described* the girl.

(pg)

GERUND
estando

PAST PARTICIPLE
estado

PRESENT
estoy
estás
está
estamos
estáis
están

PERFECT
he estado

PRESENT PROGRESSIVE
estoy estando

IMPERFECT PROGRESSIVE
estaba estando

IMPERFECT
estaba

PRETERITE
estuve
estuviste
estuvo
estuvimos
estuvisteis
estuvieron

Notes This verb looks very much like a regular **-ar** verb, and in many tenses it behaves like one. However, its irregular features are as follows:

• all forms of present indicative, present subjunctive and imperative have the stress on the (first) vowel of the ending, and so most forms need a written accent. Note the first person singular of the present indicative, **estoy**;
• the preterite is a typical **pretérito grave** type, and its stem is also used for the imperfect subjunctive.

Note also the uses of **estar** (as distinct to **ser**):

• to refer to place or location;

• to refer to the state or condition of somebody or something;

• to describe a state resulting from an action or event;

• to form the present progressive continuous.

[➤Berlitz *Spanish Grammar Handbook* for full treatment.]

IMPERATIVE

(tú) está	(vosotros) estad
(usted) esté	(ustedes) estén

PLUPERFECT
había estado

PAST ANTERIOR
hube estado

FUTURE
estaré

FUTURE PERFECT
habré estado

CONDITIONAL
estaría

CONDITIONAL PERFECT
habría/hubiera estado

PRESENT SUBJUNCTIVE
esté
estés
esté
estemos
estéis
estén

PERFECT SUBJUNCTIVE
haya estado

IMPERFECT SUBJUNCTIVE
estuviera/estuviese

PLUPERFECT SUBJUNCTIVE
hubiera/hubiese estado

¿Dónde *está* tu madre?	Where *is* your mother?
***Estuviste* allí el año pasado.**	*You were* there last year.
***Estaban* allí cuando los vi.**	*They were* there when I saw them.
***Estábamos* viendo la televisión cuando llamaste.**	*We were* watching television when you called.

GERUND
friendo

PAST PARTICIPLE
frito

PRESENT
frío
fríes
fríe
freímos
freís
fríen

PERFECT
he frito

PRESENT PROGRESSIVE
estoy friendo

IMPERFECT PROGRESSIVE
estaba friendo

IMPERFECT
freía
freías
freía
freíamos
freíais
freían

PRETERITE
freí
freíste
frió
freímos
freísteis
frieron

Notes Largely a type 3 stem-changing verb, but with the following additional irregularities:

- the accent needed whenever the **-i-** is stressed;
- the past participle.

IMPERATIVE

(tú) fríe
(usted) fría
(vosotros) freíd
(ustedes) frían

PLUPERFECT

había frito

PAST ANTERIOR

hube frito

FUTURE

freiré

FUTURE PERFECT

habré frito

CONDITIONAL

freiría

CONDITIONAL PERFECT

habría/hubiera frito

PRESENT SUBJUNCTIVE

fría
frías
fría
friamos
friais
frían

PERFECT SUBJUNCTIVE

haya frito

IMPERFECT SUBJUNCTIVE

friera/friese

PLUPERFECT SUBJUNCTIVE

hubiera/hubiese frito

Receta: Pescado *frito* con patatas *fritas*
Lava y pela las patatas, córtalas y *fríelas* en una sárten grande. Lava el pescado y córtalo en filetes; es mejor *freírlo* rebozado o empanado.

Recipe: *Fried* fish and chips

Wash and peel the potatoes, cut them up and *fry them* in a large frying pan. Wash the fish and cut it into fillets; it is best to *fry* it in batter or breadcrumbs.

(pg)

GERUND	***PAST PARTICIPLE***
habiendo	habido

PRESENT
he
has
ha
hemos
habéis
han
(hay = there is/are)

PERFECT
he habido

PRESENT PROGRESSIVE
estoy habiendo

IMPERFECT PROGRESSIVE
estaba habiendo

IMPERFECT
había

PRETERITE
hube
hubiste
hubo
hubimos
hubisteis
hubieron

Notes In some tenses, this is like a regular **-er** verb, but it is irregular in the following respects:

- the form **hay** is used for '*there is/are*' in present tense, while in other tenses the normal third person singular form is used for '*there was/were*', etc.;
- this verb has a **pretérito grave**, with **hub-** as its stem. This is also used in the imperfect subjunctive;
- the future tense stem is irregular: **habr-**;
- the present subjunctive is very irregular, with the stem **hay-**;
- this verb is very important for its use as the one and only auxiliary verb used in Spanish for the following compound tenses: perfect, pluperfect, past anterior, future perfect, conditional perfect, perfect subjunctive and pluperfect subjunctive.

IMPERATIVE
not used

PLUPERFECT
había habido

PAST ANTERIOR
hube habido

FUTURE
habré

FUTURE PERFECT
habré habido

CONDITIONAL
habría

CONDITIONAL PERFECT
habría/hubiera habido

PRESENT SUBJUNCTIVE
haya
hayas
haya
hayamos
hayáis
hayan

PERFECT SUBJUNCTIVE
haya habido

IMPERFECT SUBJUNCTIVE
hubiera/hubiese

PLUPERFECT SUBJUNCTIVE
hubiera/hubiese habido

De postre, *hay* fruta del tiempo.	For dessert *there's* fresh fruit.
¡Vamos, de prisa, *ha habido* un accidente!	Let's go, quickly, *there has been* an accident!
***Han* llegado mis amigos.**	My friends *have* arrived.
***Habíamos* pagado mil pesetas.**	We *had* paid a thousand pesetas.

(pg)

GERUND	*PAST PARTICIPLE*
haciendo	hecho

PRESENT	*PERFECT*
hago haces hace hacemos hacéis hacen	he hecho
PRESENT PROGRESSIVE	***IMPERFECT PROGRESSIVE***
estoy haciendo	estaba haciendo
IMPERFECT	***PRETERITE***
hacía	hice hiciste hizo hicimos hicisteis hicieron

Similar verbs

contrahacer	copy, imitate	**rehacer**	redo, remake
deshacer	undo, ruin	**satisfacer**	satisfy

Notes In some tenses, this is like a regular **-er** verb, but it is irregular in the following respects:

- it has a **pretérito grave**, with **hic-** as its stem (but note **hizo**: the **-c-** changes to **-z-** to keep the sound the same in front of the **-o**). This stem **hic-** is also used in the imperfect subjunctive;
- the future tense stem is irregular: **har-**;
- the first person singular of the present tense has the stem **hag-**, and this is used throughout the present subjunctive;
- the past participle is irregular (**hecho**) and is similar to that of **decir** (**dicho**).

IMPERATIVE

(tú) haz
(usted) haga
(vosotros) haced
(ustedes) hagan

PLUPERFECT
había hecho

PAST ANTERIOR
hube hecho

FUTURE
haré

FUTURE PERFECT
habré hecho

CONDITIONAL
haría

CONDITIONAL PERFECT
habría/hubiera hecho

PRESENT SUBJUNCTIVE
haga
hagas
haga
hagamos
hagáis
hagan

PERFECT SUBJUNCTIVE
haya hecho

IMPERFECT SUBJUNCTIVE
hiciera/hiciese

PLUPERFECT SUBJUNCTIVE
hubiera/hubiese hecho

¡Dicho y *hecho*! ¿Estás *satisfecho*?	No sooner said than *done*! Are you *satisfied*?
¿Qué *hacías* cuando te vi anoche?	What *were you doing* when I saw you last night?
¡Vete a *hacer* tus deberes!	Go and *do* your homework!
***Hazme* un gran favor – ¡cállate!**	*Do* me a big favor – shut up!
José-María *hizo* reparar el coche.	José-María *had* the car fixed.

GERUND	***PAST PARTICIPLE***
yendo	ido

PRESENT
voy
vas
va
vamos
vais
van

PERFECT
he ido

PRESENT PROGRESSIVE
estoy yendo

IMPERFECT PROGRESSIVE
estaba yendo

IMPERFECT
iba
ibas
iba
íbamos
ibais
iban

PRETERITE
fui
fuiste
fue
fuimos
fuisteis
fueron

Notes A highly irregular verb, although the patterns of verb endings are often very similar to, or even the same as, more regular verbs. The important first stage in mastering this verb is to be able to recognize and use correctly the various different stems. The future and conditional tenses and the past participle are regular. Other major features are:

- present indicative stem **v-** with **-ar** type endings – note first person singular form (**voy**);
- present subjunctive stem **vay-**;
- imperfect irregular, but similar to **-ar** verb pattern;
- preterite and imperfect subjunctive based on the stem **fu-**, both sets of forms being shared with **ser.**

Note that this verb is used to form the future immediate: e.g., **Mañana vamos a ir de compras** (Tomorrow we are going to go shopping).

IMPERATIVE
(tú) ve
(usted) vaya
(vosotros) id
(ustedes) vayan

PLUPERFECT
había ido

PAST ANTERIOR
hube ido

FUTURE
iré

FUTURE PERFECT
habré ido

CONDITIONAL
iría

CONDITIONAL PERFECT
habría/hubiera ido

PRESENT SUBJUNCTIVE
vaya
vayas
vaya
vayamos
vayáis
vayan

PERFECT SUBJUNCTIVE
haya ido

IMPERFECT SUBJUNCTIVE
fuera/fuese

PLUPERFECT SUBJUNCTIVE
hubiera/hubiese ido

¡*Vamos* de vacaciones!
Niños, mañana *vamos* de vacaciones. La semana pasada, papá *fue* a comprar los billetes. Ahora mismo *voy* a hacer las maletas, y pronto papá *va* a llegar a casa. Vuestra tía y vuestros primos ya han *ido* a la playa en coche, de manera que *iremos* en tren con vuestro tío. Y ahora, chicos, *id* a bañaros, y María, *vete* a la cama ya, pues ¡*vamos* a tener que levantarnos temprano!

***We're going* on vacation!**
Children, tomorrow *we are going* on vacation. Last week, Dad *went* to buy the tickets. I'm just about to pack the suitcases, and Dad *is going* to be home soon. Your aunt and your cousins have already *gone* to the shore by car, so *we will go* by train with your uncle. Now, boys, *go* and have a bath, and Maria, *go* to bed now; *we are going* to have to get up early!

GERUND	*PAST PARTICIPLE*
luciendo	lucido

PRESENT
luzco
luces
luce
lucimos
lucís
lucen

PERFECT
he lucido

PRESENT PROGRESSIVE
estoy luciendo

IMPERFECT PROGRESSIVE
estaba luciendo

IMPERFECT
lucía

PRETERITE
lucí
lucisteis
lució
lucimos
lucisteis
lucieron

Similar verb

relucir shine

Notes This verb and its compound **relucir** behave very much like **conducir** and its family, except that it does not have a **pretérito grave**. Thus the first person singular of the present indicative and all forms of the present subjunctive have the stem **luzc-**.

IMPERATIVE

(tú) luce
(usted) luzca
(vosotros) lucid
(ustedes) luzcan

PLUPERFECT

había lucido

PAST ANTERIOR

hube lucido

FUTURE

luciré

FUTURE PERFECT

habré lucido

CONDITIONAL

luciría

CONDITIONAL PERFECT

habría/hubiera lucido

PRESENT SUBJUNCTIVE

luzca
luzcas
luzca
luczamos
luzcáis
luzcan

PERFECT SUBJUNCTIVE

haya lucido

IMPERFECT SUBJUNCTIVE

luciera/luciese

PLUPERFECT SUBJUNCTIVE

hubiera/hubiese lucido

Miles de estrellas *lucen* en el cielo de Villialba.	Thousands of stars *shone* in the sky above Villialba.
Mi amiga *lució* su vestido nuevo.	My girlfriend *showed off* her new dress.

GERUND	*PAST PARTICIPLE*
oyendo	oído

PRESENT
oigo
oyes
oye
oímos
oís
oyen

PERFECT
he oído

PRESENT PROGRESSIVE
estoy oyendo

IMPERFECT PROGRESSIVE
estaba oyendo

IMPERFECT
oía

PRETERITE
oí
oíste
oyó
oímos
oísteis
oyeron

Similar verbs

desoír ignore, turn a deaf ear

Notes The irregularities:

- the **-i-** of the stem takes an accent when stressed (it is not stressed in **oiga**, the present subjunctive, the future or the conditional);
- forms with an ending beginning with **-e-** take a **-y-** to avoid three vowels coming together;
- the first person singular of the present tense has a **-g-**, which carries into all forms of the present subjunctive.

IMPERATIVE

(tú) oye	(vosotros) oíd
(usted) oiga	(ustedes) oigan

PLUPERFECT
había oído

PAST ANTERIOR
hube oído

FUTURE
oiré

FUTURE PERFECT
habré oído

CONDITIONAL
oiría

CONDITIONAL PERFECT
habría/hubiera oído

PRESENT SUBJUNCTIVE
oiga
oigas
oiga
oigamos
oigáis
oigan

PERFECT SUBJUNCTIVE
haya oído

IMPERFECT SUBJUNCTIVE
oyera/oyese

PLUPERFECT SUBJUNCTIVE
hubiera/hubiese oído

¡Habla más fuerte, no te *oigo*!	Speak up, *I* can't *hear* you!
***Oiga* usted: ¡no debe hacer eso!**	*Listen,* you mustn't do that!
¡*Oiga*! . . . ¡*Oígame*! ¿Me *oye* o no?	*Hello*! *Hello*! *Can you hear* me or not? (*on telephone*)
Llamé a mi hija, pero no me *oyó*.	I called my daughter, but *she* didn't *hear* me.
¿No me escuchas, o es que no me *oyes*, o qué?	Aren't you listening to me, or can't *you hear* me, or what?

GERUND	*PAST PARTICIPLE*
oliendo	olido

PRESENT	*PERFECT*
huelo	he olido
hueles	
huele	
olemos	
oléis	
huelen	

PRESENT PROGRESSIVE	*IMPERFECT PROGRESSIVE*
estoy oliendo	estaba oliendo

IMPERFECT	*PRETERITE*
olía	olí
olías	oliste
olía	olió
olíamos	olimos
olíais	olisteis
olían	olieron

Notes **Oler** is a predictable type 1 stem-changing verb with a particular oddity: it has **o-** changing to **-ue-** when the stem is stressed, but the **-ue-** is always preceded by **h-**, so that forms in which the stem is stressed begin with **hue-**. In other respects it is a normal stem-changing verb.

IMPERATIVE
(tú) huele
(usted) huela
(vosotros) oled
(ustedes) huelan

PLUPERFECT
había olido

PAST ANTERIOR
hube olido

FUTURE
oleré

FUTURE PERFECT
habré olido

CONDITIONAL
olería

CONDITIONAL PERFECT
habría/hubiera olido

PRESENT SUBJUNCTIVE
huela
huelas
huela
olamos
oláis
huelan

PERFECT SUBJUNCTIVE
haya olido

IMPERFECT SUBJUNCTIVE
oliera/oliese

PLUPERFECT SUBJUNCTIVE
hubiera/hubiese olido

Este pastel *huele* a quemado.	This cake *smells* burnt.
¡Qué bien *huelen* estas manzanas!	Don't these apples *smell* good!
La habitación *olía* a jazmín.	The room *smelled* of jasmine.
De repente los perros *olieron* el zorro.	Suddenly the dogs *smelled* the fox.
Muchachos, ¡*oled* esto! Parece estar podrido.	Boys, *smell* this! It seems to be rotten.

46 poder be able, can

(pg)

GERUND	***PAST PARTICIPLE***
pudiendo	podido

PRESENT
puedo
puedes
puede
podemos
podéis
pueden

PERFECT
he podido

PRESENT PROGRESSIVE
estoy pudiendo

IMPERFECT PROGRESSIVE
estaba pudiendo

IMPERFECT
podía

PRETERITE
pude
pudiste
pudo
pudimos
pudisteis
pudieron

Notes This verb has the following irregularities:

- the stem changes in the present indicative and subjunctive are those of a type 1 **o→ e** stem-changing verb;
- this is a **pretérito grave** verb, with the stem **pud-**, which also carries over into the imperfect subjunctive;
- in addition, **poder** has **pudiendo** as its gerund;
- the future and conditional stem loses the **-e-** of the infinitive, becoming **podr-**.

IMPERATIVE
not used

PLUPERFECT
había podido

PAST ANTERIOR
hube podido

FUTURE
podré

FUTURE PERFECT
habré podido

CONDITIONAL
podría

CONDITIONAL PERFECT
habría/hubiera podido

PRESENT SUBJUNCTIVE
pueda
puedas
pueda
podamos
podáis
puedan

PERFECT SUBJUNCTIVE
haya podido

IMPERFECT SUBJUNCTIVE
pudiera/pudiese

PLUPERFECT SUBJUNCTIVE
hubiera/hubiese podido

¿Se *puede* telefonear de aquí?	*Can* one telephone from here?
Huy, gracias, ¡pero no *puedo* más! Ya estoy harto.	Thanks, but *I can't* manage any more! I'm full up.
Los alpinistas *no pudieron* llegar hasta la cima a causa de la nieve.	The mountaineers *were unable* to get to the top because of the snow.
¡*No podría* sobrevivir sin ti!	I *couldn't* survive without you!
Mañana *podréis* ver el mar por primera vez.	Tomorrow *you will be able* to see the sea for the first time.

(pg)

GERUND	***PAST PARTICIPLE***
poniendo	puesto

PRESENT
pongo
pones
pone
ponemos
ponéis
ponen

PERFECT
he puesto

PRESENT PROGRESSIVE
estoy poniendo

IMPERFECT PROGRESSIVE
estaba poniendo

IMPERFECT
ponía

PRETERITE
puse
pusiste
puso
pusimos
pusisteis
pusieron

Similar verbs

componer	compose	**posponer**	postpone
descomponer	decompose	**proponer**	propose
disponer	dispose, break down	**reponerse**	get fit, recover
imponer	impose	**suponer**	suppose
indisponer	indispose	**trasponer**	transpose
oponer	oppose		

Notes This highly irregular verb has the following features:

- the first person singular of the present tense, and therefore all of the present subjunctive, have the stem **pong-**;
- the preterite is **pretérito grave**, with the stem **pus-**, which is also used in the imperfect subjunctive;
- the past participle is irregular (**puesto**);
- the singular informal/familiar imperative is **pon**;
- the stem for the future and conditional is **pondr-**.

IMPERATIVE
(tú) pon
(usted) ponga
(vosotros) poned
(ustedes) pongan

PLUPERFECT
había puesto

PAST ANTERIOR
hube puesto

FUTURE
pondré

FUTURE PERFECT
habré puesto

CONDITIONAL
pondría

CONDITIONAL PERFECT
habría/hubiera puesto

PRESENT SUBJUNCTIVE
ponga
pongas
ponga
pongamos
pongáis
pongan

PERFECT SUBJUNCTIVE
haya puesto

IMPERFECT SUBJUNCTIVE
pusiera/pusiese

PLUPERFECT SUBJUNCTIVE
hubiera/hubiese puesto

Nos mudamos de casa
Querida, vamos a *poner* las plantas en tu coche, ¿no? Ya he *puesto* las maletas en el mío . . . Sí, señor, *ponga* la mesa en el camión. Al llegar, *pondremos* todas las sillas en el comedor, ¿vale? ¿Dónde están las llaves de la casa? Creo que las *puse* en el coche. Miguel, *ponte* el abrigo . . . hace frío.

We move
Darling, we're going to *put* the plants in your car, aren't we? I've already *put* the suitcases in mine. Yes, *put* the table in the truck. When we arrive, *we'll put* all the chairs in the dining room, OK? Where are the keys to the house? I think *I put* them in the car. Michael, *put* your coat on . . . it's cold.

(pg)

GERUND	***PAST PARTICIPLE***
queriendo	querido

PRESENT
quiero
quieres
quiere
queremos
queréis
quieren

PERFECT
he querido

PRESENT PROGRESSIVE
estoy queriendo

IMPERFECT PROGRESSIVE
estaba queriendo

IMPERFECT
quería

PRETERITE
quise
quisiste
quiso
quisimos
quisisteis
quisieron

Notes This verb has the following irregularities:

- it is basically a stem-changing verb with **-e-** changing to **-ie-** when stressed;
- in addition, **querer** has a **pretérito grave** with the stem **quis-**, also used in the imperfect subjunctive;
- the future and conditional stem is **querr-**.

IMPERATIVE

(tú) quiere
(usted) quiera

(vosotros) quered
(ustedes) quieran

PLUPERFECT
había querido

PAST ANTERIOR
hube querido

FUTURE
querré

FUTURE PERFECT
habré querido

CONDITIONAL
querría

CONDITIONAL PERFECT
habría/hubiera querido

PRESENT SUBJUNCTIVE
quiera
quieras
quiera
queramos
queráis
quieran

PERFECT SUBJUNCTIVE
haya querido

IMPERFECT SUBJUNCTIVE
quisiera/quisiese

PLUPERFECT SUBJUNCTIVE
hubiera/hubiese querido

Lo hice sin *querer*.	I did it without *meaning to.*
Te *quiero* más que tú me *quieres* a mí.	*I love* you more than *you love* me.
¡*Queremos* pan!	*We want* some bread!
Tienes que hacerlo, *quieras* o no.	You have to do it whether *you like* it or not.
Al saber que hacía mal tiempo, no *quisieron* salir de casa.	When they found out that the weather was bad, *they were unwilling* (*decided not*) to go out.
***Quisiéramos* ver Granada en primavera.**	*We'd like* to see Granada in the spring.

GERUND	***PAST PARTICIPLE***
riendo	reído

PRESENT
río
ríes
ríe
reímos
reís
ríen

PERFECT
he reído

PRESENT PROGRESSIVE
estoy riendo

IMPERFECT PROGRESSIVE
estaba riendo

IMPERFECT
reía

PRETERITE
reí
reiste
rió
reímos
reísteis
rieron

Similar verb

sonreír smile

Note This verb is actually a type 3 stem-changing verb like **pedir**, but any form with a stressed **-i-** needs an accent.

IMPERATIVE

(tú) ríe	(vosotros) reíd
(usted) ría	(ustedes) rían

PLUPERFECT
había reído

PAST ANTERIOR
hube reído

FUTURE
reiré

FUTURE PERFECT
habré reído

CONDITIONAL
reiría

CONDITIONAL PERFECT
habría/hubiera reído

PRESENT SUBJUNCTIVE
ría
rías
ría
riamos
riais
rían

PERFECT SUBJUNCTIVE
haya reído

IMPERFECT SUBJUNCTIVE
riera/riese

PLUPERFECT SUBJUNCTIVE
hubiera/hubiese reído

¡Ese muchacho me hace *reír*!	That boy makes me *laugh*!
¡No te *rías* de mí!	Don't *laugh* at me!
¡No me hagas *reír*!	Don't make me *laugh*!
***Ríete* niño, no llores más . . .**	*Laugh*, child, don't cry any more . . .
La joven me *sonrió* antes de salir.	The young girl *smiled* at me before going out.
No os *riáis* de él/No se *rían* de él.	Don't *laugh* at him.
Se fue, *riendo* a más no poder.	He went off *laughing* for all he was worth.
***Rió* el último.**	He had the last *laugh*.
***Reían* como locos.**	*They were laughing* like mad.

GERUND	*PAST PARTICIPLE*
rompiendo	roto

PRESENT
rompo
rompes
rompe
rompemos
rompéis
rompen

PERFECT
he roto

PRESENT PROGRESSIVE
estoy rompiendo

IMPERFECT PROGRESSIVE
estaba rompiendo

IMPERFECT
rompía

PRETERITE
rompí
rompiste
rompió
rompimos
rompisties
rompieron

Note This verb's only irregularity is its past participle, **roto**.

IMPERATIVE
(tú) rompe
(usted) rompa
(vosotros) romped
(ustedes) rompan

PLUPERFECT
había roto

PAST ANTERIOR
hube roto

FUTURE
romperé

FUTURE PERFECT
habré roto

CONDITIONAL
rompería

CONDITIONAL PERFECT
habría/hubiera roto

PRESENT SUBJUNCTIVE
rompa
rompas
rompa
rompamos
rompáis
rompan

PERFECT SUBJUNCTIVE
haya roto

IMPERFECT SUBJUNCTIVE
rompiera/rompiese

PLUPERFECT SUBJUNCTIVE
hubiera/hubiese roto

Esta mujer se *rompió* la pierna en el accidente.	This woman *broke* her leg in the accident.
¡No me *rompas* el boli!	Don't *break* my ballpoint!
Todas las ventanas estaban *rotas*.	All of the windows were *broken*.
Se *rompieron* las botellas.	The bottles *got broken*.

(pg)

GERUND	*PAST PARTICIPLE*
sabiendo	sabido

PRESENT
sé
sabes
sabe
sabemos
sabéis
saben

PERFECT
he sabido

PRESENT PROGRESSIVE
estoy sabiendo

IMPERFECT PROGRESSIVE
estaba sabiendo

IMPERFECT
sabía

PRETERITE
supe
supiste
supo
supimos
supisteis
supieron

Notes This verb has four elements of irregularity:

- the first person singular of the present indicative, **sé**;
- the whole of the present subjunctive, based on the stem **sep-**;
- the **pretérito grave** with the stem **sup-**, also used for the imperfect subjunctive;
- the future tense stem **sabr-**, also used in the conditional.

Note that this verb is used for *to be able to, can* when 'knowing how to do something' is implied.

IMPERATIVE
(tú) sabe
(usted) sepa
(vosotros) sabed
(ustedes) sepan

PLUPERFECT
había sabido

PAST ANTERIOR
hube sabido

FUTURE
sabré

FUTURE PERFECT
habré sabido

CONDITIONAL
sabría

CONDITIONAL PERFECT
habría/hubiera sabido

PRESENT SUBJUNCTIVE
sepa
sepas
sepa
sepamos
sepáis
sepan

PERFECT SUBJUNCTIVE
haya sabido

IMPERFECT SUBJUNCTIVE
supiera/supiese

PLUPERFECT SUBJUNCTIVE
hubiera/hubiese sabido

Pero, ¡no *sabes* nada!	But, you don't *know* anything!
Que yo *sepa*, tendría unos diez años.	As far as I *know*, he'd be about ten years old.
***Sabéis* esquiar, ¿verdad?**	*You do know how to* ski, don't you?
Al llegar a casa, *supe* que había muerto mi tía.	When I got home, *I learned* that my aunt had died.
Sí, sí, ya lo *sé*.	Yes, yes, *I know.*

GERUND	*PAST PARTICIPLE*
saliendo	salido

PRESENT
salgo
sales
sale
salimos
salís
salen

PERFECT
he salido

PRESENT PROGRESSIVE
estoy saliendo

IMPERFECT PROGRESSIVE
estaba saliendo

IMPERFECT
salía

PRETERITE
salí
saliste
salió
salimos
salisteis
salieron

Notes The three irregular features are as follows:

- the first person singular of the present indicative, and so all of the present subjunctive, which have the stem **salg-**;
- the familiar singular imperative is **sal**;
- the irregular stem **saldr-**, used for the future and conditional.

IMPERATIVE

(tú) sal
(usted) salga
(vosotros) salid
(ustedes) salgan

PLUPERFECT

había salido

PAST ANTERIOR

hube salido

FUTURE

saldré

FUTURE PERFECT

habré salido

CONDITIONAL

saldría

CONDITIONAL PERFECT

habría/hubiera salido

PRESENT SUBJUNCTIVE

salga
salgas
salga
salgamos
salgáis
salgan

PERFECT SUBJUNCTIVE

haya salido

IMPERFECT SUBJUNCTIVE

saliera/saliese

PLUPERFECT SUBJUNCTIVE

hubiera/hubiese salido

¡*Sal* de ahí, idiota!	*Get out* of there, you idiot!
No *salgo* mucho, pues no tengo tiempo, pero *saldremos* mañana si quieres.	*I* don't *go out* much, I don't have time, but *we'll go out* tomorrow if you like.
***Salgan* con cuidado, por favor.**	*Go/get out* carefully, please.
Oye, ¿quieres *salir* conmigo?	Hey, do you want to *go out* with me?

GERUND	*PAST PARTICIPLE*
siendo	sido

PRESENT
soy
eres
es
somos
sois
son

PERFECT
he sido

PRESENT PROGRESSIVE
estoy siendo

IMPERFECT PROGRESSIVE
estaba siendo

IMPERFECT
era
eras
era
éramos
erais
eran

PRETERITE
fui
fuiste
fue
fuimos
fuisteis
fueron

Notes This highly irregular verb should be learned thoroughly, noting the following features:

• the first person singular of the present tense is **soy**, and the rest of the forms of this tense are highly irregular, as with the imperative forms;
• the present subjunctive is based on the form **sea**;
• the preterite is highly irregular, and its stem is used for the imperfect subjunctive (in both of these, **ser** shares its forms with **ir**);
• the imperfect is based on the form **era**;
• several other forms are apparently regular – the gerund, the past participle, the future and the conditional.

Note also that **ser** is used to form the passive, together with the past participle of the main verb [➤*The verb system in Spanish*].

IMPERATIVE

(tú) sé
(usted) sea
(vosotros) sed
(ustedes) sean

PLUPERFECT
había sido

PAST ANTERIOR
hube sido

FUTURE
seré

FUTURE PERFECT
habré sido

CONDITIONAL
sería

CONDITIONAL PERFECT
habría/hubiera sido

PRESENT SUBJUNCTIVE
sea
seas
sea
seamos
seáis
sean

PERFECT SUBJUNCTIVE
haya sido

IMPERFECT SUBJUNCTIVE
fuera/fuese

PLUPERFECT SUBJUNCTIVE
hubiera/hubiese sido

¡*Sé* bueno, o me enfadaré contigo!	*Be* good or I'll get angry with you!
***Somos* amigos desde hace años.**	*We've been* friends for years.
***Eran* las dos de la tarde.**	*It was* two o'clock in the afternoon.
***Soy* soltero, ¡pero que no lo *sea* siempre!**	*I'm* a bachelor, but may I not always *be*!
***Fueron* cinco niños los que sufrieron.**	*It was* five children who suffered.
Había *sido* profesor, pero ya no lo *era*.	He had *been* a teacher, but *was* no longer.

54 tener — have

(pg)

GERUND	**PAST PARTICIPLE**
teniendo	tenido

PRESENT
tengo
tienes
tiene
tenemos
tenéis
tienen

PERFECT
he tenido

PRESENT PROGRESSIVE
estoy teniendo

IMPERFECT PROGRESSIVE
estaba teniendo

IMPERFECT
tenía

PRETERITE
tuve
tuviste
tuvo
tuvimos
tuvisteis
tuvieron

Similar verbs

abstener(se)	abstain	**entretener**	entertain
contener	contain	**mantener**	maintain
detener	detain, arrest	**obtener**	obtain
sostener	sustain		

Notes The main irregular features are as follows:

- the first person singular of the present tense is **tengo**, and so the present subjunctive has the stem **teng-**;
- the rest of the present indicative behaves like an **e → ie** stem-changing verb;
- the **pretérito grave** stem is **tuv-**, also used for the imperfect subjunctive;
- the future and conditional stem is **tendr-**;
- the familiar singular imperative is **ten**.

IMPERATIVE
(tú) ten
(usted) tenga
(vosotros) tened
(ustedes) tengan

PLUPERFECT
había tenido

PAST ANTERIOR
hube tenido

FUTURE
tendré

FUTURE PERFECT
habré tenido

CONDITIONAL
tendría

CONDITIONAL PERFECT
habría/hubiera tenido

PRESENT SUBJUNCTIVE
tenga
tengas
tenga
tengamos
tengáis
tengan

PERFECT SUBJUNCTIVE
haya tenido

IMPERFECT SUBJUNCTIVE
tuviera/tuviese

PLUPERFECT SUBJUNCTIVE
hubiera/hubiese tenido

¡*Ten* cuidado! Es peligroso asomarse.	*Be* careful! It's dangerous to lean out.
***Tenemos* prisa, ¡venga, corre!**	*We're in* a hurry, come on run!
***Tenga* piedad de nosotros.**	*Have* mercy on us.
Ha *tenido* mucho que hacer.	She has *had* a lot to do.
***Teníamos* mucho frío.**	*We were* very cold.
***Tuvieron* que salir.**	*They had* to go out.
Quien *tuviera* dinero lo compraría.	Whoever *had* enough money would buy it.

(pg)

GERUND	*PAST PARTICIPLE*
trayendo	traído

PRESENT
traigo
traes
trae
traemos
traéis
traen

PERFECT
he traído

PRESENT PROGRESSIVE
estoy trayendo

IMPERFECT PROGRESSIVE
estaba trayendo

IMPERFECT
traía

PRETERITE
traje
trajiste
trajo
trajimos
trajisteis
trajeron

Similar verbs

atraer	attract	**distraer**	distract
contraer	contract	**sustraer**	subtract

Notes The irregular features are as follows:

- the first person singular of the present indicative is **traigo**, giving the present subjunctive stem **traig-**;
- the **pretérito grave** stem is **traj-**, used also for the imperfect subjunctive; note the missing **-i-** of the third person plural;
- any form with an ending beginning with **-i-** has a **-y-** instead (except for the third person plural of the preterite, as explained above);
- the **-i-** of the past participle needs an accent.

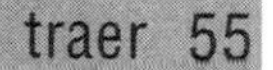

IMPERATIVE
(tú) trae
(usted) traiga
(vosotros) traed
(ustedes) traigan

PLUPERFECT
había traído

PAST ANTERIOR
hube traído

FUTURE
traeré

FUTURE PERFECT
habré traído

CONDITIONAL
traería

CONDITIONAL PERFECT
habría/hubiera traído

PRESENT SUBJUNCTIVE
traiga
traigas
traiga
traigamos
traigáis
traigan

PERFECT SUBJUNCTIVE
haya traído

IMPERFECT SUBJUNCTIVE
trajera/trajese

PLUPERFECT SUBJUNCTIVE
hubiera/hubiese traído

Tráigame **más pan, por favor.**	*Bring me* more bread, please.
Traje **sólo dos mil pesetas.**	*I* only *brought* two thousand pesetas.
Los niños me ***traían*** **sus deberes.**	The children *used to bring* me their homework.
¿Han ***traído*** **sus cartas?**	Have you *brought* your letters?

GERUND	*PAST PARTICIPLE*
valiendo	valido

PRESENT
valgo
vales
vale
valemos
valéis
valen

PERFECT
he valido

PRESENT PROGRESSIVE
estoy valiendo

IMPERFECT PROGRESSIVE
estaba valiendo

IMPERFECT
valía

PRETERITE
valí
valiste
valió
valimos
valisteis
valieron

Notes The only irregular features are:

- the first person singular of the present indicative is **valgo**, giving the present subjunctive stem **valg-**;
- the stem of the future and conditional is **valdr-**.

IMPERATIVE
(tú) vale
(usted) valga
(vosotros) valed
(ustedes) valgan

PLUPERFECT
había valido

PAST ANTERIOR
hube valido

FUTURE
valdré

FUTURE PERFECT
habré valido

CONDITIONAL
valdría

CONDITIONAL PERFECT
habría/hubiera valido

PRESENT SUBJUNCTIVE
valga
valgas
valga
valgamos
valgáis
valgan

PERFECT SUBJUNCTIVE
haya valido

IMPERFECT SUBJUNCTIVE
valiera/valiese

PLUPERFECT SUBJUNCTIVE
hubiera/hubiese valido

No *vale* la pena volver.	*It's* not *worth* coming back.
Estas camisas *valían* cinco mil pesetas.	These shirts *were worth* five thousand pesetas.

(pg)

GERUND	PAST PARTICIPLE
viniendo	venido

PRESENT
vengo
vienes
viene
venimos
venís
vienen

PERFECT
he venido

PRESENT PROGRESSIVE
estoy viniendo

IMPERFECT PROGRESSIVE
estaba viniendo

IMPERFECT
venía

PRETERITE
vine
viniste
vino
vinimos
vinisteis
vinieron

Similar verbs

contravenir	contravene	**intervenir**	intervene
convenir	fit, suit		

Notes The main irregular features are as follows:

- the first person singular of the present tense is **vengo**, so the present subjunctive has the stem **veng-**;
- the rest of the present indicative behaves like an **e → ie** stem-changing verb;
- the **pretérito grave** stem is **vin-**, also used for the imperfect subjunctive and the gerund;
- the future and conditional stem is **vendr-**;
- the familiar singular imperative is **ven**.

IMPERATIVE

(tú) ven
(usted) venga
(vosotros) venid
(ustedes) vengan

PLUPERFECT

había venido

PAST ANTERIOR

hube venido

FUTURE

vendré

FUTURE PERFECT

habré venido

CONDITIONAL

vendría

CONDITIONAL PERFECT

habría/hubiera venido

PRESENT SUBJUNCTIVE

venga
vengas
venga
vengamos
vengáis
vengan

PERFECT SUBJUNCTIVE

haya venido

IMPERFECT SUBJUNCTIVE

viniera/viniese

PLUPERFECT SUBJUNCTIVE

hubiera/hubiese venido

***Venga* conmigo a la comisaría.**	*Come* with me to the police station.
***Vinieron* en el tren de las doce.**	*They came* on the twelve o'clock train.
***Venía* al colegio todos los días.**	*He came* to school every day.
***Vendremos* a verte mañana.**	*We'll come* and see you tomorrow.

GERUND	***PAST PARTICIPLE***
viendo	visto

PRESENT
veo
ves
ve
vemos
veis
ven

PERFECT
he visto

PRESENT PROGRESSIVE
estoy viendo

IMPERFECT PROGRESSIVE
estaba viendo

IMPERFECT
veía

PRETERITE
vi
viste
vio
vimos
visteis
vieron

Similar verbs

entrever	glimpse	**prever**	foresee, plan

Notes The main irregular features are:

- the stem of the first person singular of the present indicative, all of the present subjunctive and the imperfect indicative is **ve-**;
- the preterite forms are as for **-er** and **-ir** verbs, but with no written accents;
- the past participle is irregular: **visto**.

In other respects, **ver** is regular, but note that the familiar singular imperative – **ve** – is identical to that of **ir** 'to go'.

IMPERATIVE
(tú) ve
(usted) vea
(vosotros) ved
(ustedes) vean

PLUPERFECT
había visto

PAST ANTERIOR
hube visto

FUTURE
veré

FUTURE PERFECT
habré visto

CONDITIONAL
vería

CONDITIONAL PERFECT
habría/hubiera visto

PRESENT SUBJUNCTIVE
vea
veas
vea
veamos
veáis
vean

PERFECT SUBJUNCTIVE
haya visto

IMPERFECT SUBJUNCTIVE
viera/viese

PLUPERFECT SUBJUNCTIVE
hubiera/hubiese visto

¡Te *veo* muy bien!	*I can see* you clearly!
Nos *vieron* entrar en el café.	*They saw* us/we *were seen* going into the cafe.
***Veíamos* que no estaban allí.**	*We could see* that they were not there.
Había *visto* a su madre en casa.	He had *seen* his mother at home.

C
SUBJECT INDEX

The references given are to the relevant section in *The verb system in Spanish*.

D

VERB INDEX

An asterisk before a verb indicates that it is one of the Model Verbs listed in section B.

Where **ch**, **ll** and **ñ** are concerned, English alphabetical order has been used throughout.

A

abandonar *(tr)*	abandon, desert, leave behind	**2**
abastecer *(tr)*	supply, provide	**32**
ablandar *(tr)*	soften	**2**
abolir *(tr)*	abolish	**4**
abordar *(tr)*	accost	**2**
aborrecer *(tr)*	hate	**32**
abortar *(intr)*	miscarry	**2**
abotonar *(tr)*	button	**2**
abrasar *(tr)*	scorch	**2**
abrazar(se) *(tr/refl)*	embrace, cuddle	**6**
abrevar *(tr)*	water (*animals*)	**2**
abreviar(se) *(tr/refl)*	shorten, become shorter	**14**
abrigar(se) *(tr/refl)*	shelter	**7**
***abrir** *(tr/intr)*	open, open out, open up	**25**
abrir *(tr)*	turn on (*faucet/tap*)	
abrir con llave *(tr)*	unlock	
abrir la cremallera *(tr)*	zip open	
abrir por fuerza *(tr)*	force one's way into	
abrir sobre *(intr)*	open onto	
abrochar *(tr)*	button, fasten	**2**
absolver *(tr)*	absolve, let off	**20**
absorber *(tr)*	absorb	**3**
abstenerse de *(refl)*	abstain from, refrain from; keep off	**54**
abultar *(tr)*	swell	**2**
abundar de/en *(intr)*	abound, be abundant	**2**
aburrir *(tr)*	bore	**4**
abusar de *(tr)*	misuse, abuse	**2**
acabar *(tr)*	finish, complete; accomplish	**2**
acabar con *(tr)*	finish with; do away with	
acabar de	have just	
acabar(se) *(intr/refl)*	stop, end, finish, complete; end up	**2**
acallar *(tr)*	silence	**2**
acampar(se) *(intr/refl)*	camp	**2**
acanalar *(tr)*	channel	**2**
acariciar *(tr)*	caress, feel, stroke, pet, fondle, cherish	**2**

acarrear *(tr)*	haul **2**
acechar *(tr)*	lie in wait for **2**
acelerar(se) *(tr/refl)*	speed up, accelerate **2**
aceptar *(tr)*	accept **2**
acerar *(tr)*	steel **2**
acercarse a *(refl)*	approach **5**
acertar *(tr/intr)*	hit the mark, succeed **19**
aclarar *(tr)*	clarify, clear up; rinse **2**
acoger *(tr)*	welcome **11**
acometer *(tr)*	attack; undertake **3**
acomodar *(tr)*	accommodate, lodge, put up; suit **2**
acompañar *(tr)*	accompany **2**
aconsejar *(tr)*	advise **2**
acontecer *(intr)*	happen, occur; chance **32**
acoplar(se) *(tr/refl)*	mate **2**
acordar *(tr)*	tune **20**
acordarse de *(refl)*	remember **20**
acortar(se) *(tr/refl)*	shorten, draw in, become shorter **2**
acosar *(tr)*	hound, harass, pester **2**
acostar *(tr)*	put to bed **20**
acostarse *(refl)*	lie (down), go to bed **20**
acostumbrar *(tr)*	accustom **2**
acostumbrarse a *(refl)*	become accustomed, get used to **2**
acribillar a *(tr)*	riddle with; pester **2**
actualizar *(tr)*	modernize, update **6**
***actuar** *(tr/intr)*	act, do, perform **15**
actuar de mimo *(intr)*	mime
acudir *(intr)*	gather around; come to help; show up, turn up **4**
acumular(se) *(tr/refl)*	accumulate, collect, mount up **2**
acunar *(tr)*	rock (to sleep) **2**
acuñar *(tr)*	strike (*coin, medal*); wedge **2**
acusar *(tr)*	accuse, charge **2**
adaptar *(tr)*	adapt; suit **2**
adaptarse a *(refl)*	adapt, adjust to **2**
adelantar *(tr/intr)*	overtake, advance, move forward **2**
adelgazar *(tr/intr)*	get thin, lose weight, reduce, slim, thin down **6**
adherirse a *(refl)*	cling to, adhere to, stick **4**
adiestrar *(tr)*	train; drill **2**
adivinar *(tr/intr)*	guess **2**

ahogar(se) *(tr/refl)*	drown; suffocate; throttle **7**
ahorrar *(tr)*	put away, put aside, save (*money*, *time*) **2**
ahuecar *(tr)*	hollow out **5**
ahusarse *(refl)*	taper **2**
aislar de *(tr)*	isolate (from) **15**
ajustar *(tr)*	adjust, adapt, regulate; settle (*accounts*); suit **2**
alabar *(tr)*	praise **2**
alargar(se) *(tr/refl)*	hold out, lengthen, draw out, stretch, extend **7**
alarmar *(tr)*	alarm, frighten, terrify **2**
alborear *(intr)*	dawn **2**
alborotar *(intr)*	make a racket, brawl **2**
alcanzar *(tr/intr)*	reach, get to, attain, hit (*target*); catch up with **6**
alejar *(tr)*	alienate, distance, keep away, push away, move away **2**
alejarse *(refl)*	go away **2**
alentar *(tr)*	encourage; breathe **2**
aligerar *(tr)*	lighten **2**
alimentar *(tr)*	feed **2**
alinear(se) *(tr/refl)*	line up, align **2**
alisar *(tr)*	flatten, smooth **2**
alistarse a *(refl)*	join up (*armed services*) **2**
aliviar *(tr)*	alleviate, relieve, comfort, deaden (*pain*) **2**
allanar *(tr)*	flatten, level, smooth **2**
almacenar *(tr)*	hoard, store; (*general, computing*) **2**
almorzar *(intr)*	have lunch **6, 20**
alojar *(tr)*	accommodate, lodge, put up, house **2**
alquilar *(tr)*	rent, rent out, hire, charter, hire out, let **2**
alterar *(tr)*	upset, disturb **2**
alternar *(intr)*	alternate **2**
aludir a *(intr)*	refer to **4**
alumbrar *(tr)*	light (up) **2**
alzar *(tr)*	hoist, raise, lift **6**
amalgamar *(tr)*	amalgamate **2**
amamantar *(tr)*	suckle **2**
amanecer *(intr)*	dawn **32**
amansar *(tr)*	tame **2**

amar *(tr)*	love **2**
amargar *(tr)*	sour **7**
amarrar *(tr)*	fasten, tie up, moor **2**
amarrar con una cuerda *(tr)*	rope together
amenazar *(tr)*	threaten **6**
amoldar *(tr)*	mold **2**
amontonar *(tr)*	heap, hoard **2**
amontonar(se) *(tr/refl)*	huddle, pile, pile up **2**
amortiguar *(tr)*	deaden, muffle **8**
amortizar *(tr)*	pay off **6**
amotinarse *(refl)*	riot **2**
ampliar *(tr)*	widen, increase, enlarge, expand **14**
amplificar *(tr)*	amplify **5**
ampollar(se) *(tr/refl)*	blister **2**
amputar *(tr)*	amputate **2**
analizar *(tr)*	analyze **6**
anclar *(intr)*	anchor **2**
***andar** *(intr)*	march, walk, go; function, work **27**
andar a gatas *(intr)*	crawl, creep
andar a pasos largos *(intr)*	stride
andar con paso majestuoso *(intr)*	sweep (*movement*)
andar por *(tr)*	haunt (*ghost*)
aneblarse *(refl)*	become misty **2**
anejar *(tr)*	annex **2**
anestesiar *(tr)*	anaesthetize **2**
anexionar *(tr)*	append **2**
anhelar *(tr)*	long for **2**
anidar *(tr/intr)*	nest **2**
animar *(tr)*	animate, encourage **2**
animarse *(refl)*	brighten up, cheer up; bear up **2**
aniquilar *(tr)*	annihilate **2**
anochecer *(intr)*	get dark **32**
anotar *(tr)*	write down **2**
anticipar *(tr)*	anticipate, advance (*payment*) **2**
anudar *(tr)*	knot **2**
anular *(tr)*	annul, cancel out, write off (*insurance*, *debt*) **2**
anunciar *(tr)*	announce, advertize, publicize **2**
añadir *(tr)*	add, annex **4**
apacentar *(tr)*	graze **2**

apaciguar *(tr)*	pacify, appease **8**
apagar *(tr)*	extinguish, put out; quench; switch off, turn off **7**
apagarse *(refl)*	go out, die away **7**
aparcar *(tr)*	park, garage **5**
aparecer *(intr)*	appear, come into sight, show up **32**
aparecer inesperadamente *(intr)*	pop up
aparentar *(tr)*	pretend **2**
apartar *(tr)*	move away **2**
apartarse de *(refl)*	diverge from **2**
apedrear *(tr)*	stone **2**
apelar a *(tr/intr)*	appeal **2**
apercibir *(tr)*	catch sight of **4**
apetecer *(tr)*	feel like, want **32**
apilar(se) *(tr/refl)*	pile, pile up **3**
aplastar *(tr)*	crush **2**
aplaudir *(tr/intr)*	applaud, clap **4**
aplazar *(tr)*	adjourn, postpone, defer, put off, delay, wait, procrastinate **6**
aplicar *(tr)*	apply **5**
aporrear *(tr)*	beat up, bash **2**
apostar *(tr/intr)*	bet, stake, bet on, back **20**
apoyar *(tr)*	hold up, side with, support, back, back (up); champion; prop, shore up; stand by, uphold **2**
apoyar(se) en *(tr/refl)*	lean (on) **2**
apreciar *(tr)*	appreciate, cherish; assess, prize, value **2**
aprender *(tr)*	learn **3**
aprender de memoria *(tr)*	learn by heart
apresurarse a *(refl)*	make haste, hurry, speed **2**
apretar(se) *(tr/refl)*	press (*button*, etc.); screw; tighten (*nut*); squeeze **19**
aprisionar *(tr)*	trap, imprison **2**
aprobar *(tr/intr)*	approve, agree to; endorse; pass (*exam*, *law*) **20**
aprovechar de *(tr)*	benefit from **2**
aproximarse a *(refl)*	approximate **2**
apuntar *(tr)*	note down, record, note, write down **2**
apuntar a *(refl)*	aim

apuñalar *(tr)*	stab **2**
arañar *(tr)*	scratch **2**
arar *(tr)*	plow/plough **2**
arbitrar en *(tr)*	referee **2**
arbitrar entre *(intr)*	arbitrate between
archivar *(tr)*	file **2**
arder *(intr)*	burn, blaze **3**
arder de *(tr)*	inflame with
armar *(tr)*	arm **2**
armonizar *(tr)*	harmonize **6**
arrancar *(intr)*	boot up (*computing*); start, start up **5**
arrancarse *(refl)*	start up **5**
arrastrar *(tr)*	haul, heave, trail, drag **2**
arrastrarse *(refl)*	crawl, creep, drag **2**
arrebatar *(tr)*	snatch **2**
arreglar *(tr)*	arrange, sort out, fix, settle; mend, regulate, repair; sort, trim, tidy up **2**
arreglárselas *(refl)*	cope **2**
arrendar *(tr)*	lease (out), rent, rent out **19**
arrepentirse de *(refl)*	regret **22**
arrestar *(tr)*	arrest **2**
arriesgar *(tr)*	chance, risk **7**
arriesgarse *(refl)*	venture, risk, dare **7**
arrodillarse *(refl)*	kneel (down) **2**
arrojar *(tr)*	fling, throw, cast, hurl, bowl, pitch **2**
arrollar *(tr/intr)*	coil, roll up **2**
arrugar(se) *(tr/refl)*	wrinkle, ruffle **7**
arruinar *(tr)*	ruin, bankrupt, make a mess of, wreck **2**
asaltar *(tr)*	assault, storm **2**
asar *(tr)*	roast **2**
asar a la parrilla *(tr)*	grill
ascender *(tr)*	promote, advance (*rank*) **19**
ascender *(intr)*	go up, ascend **19**
ascender a *(intr)*	number, amount to, add up to
asediar *(tr)*	besiege **2**
asegurar *(tr)*	assure, ensure, make safe, fasten, secure, underwrite **2**
asegurar(se) *(tr/refl)*	insure **2**

asentar *(tr/intr)*	agree **19**
asesinar *(tr)*	assassinate, murder, slaughter **2**
asfixiar(se) *(tr/refl)*	suffocate, throttle **2**
asignar *(tr)*	allocate, assign, allow **2**
asimilar *(tr)*	assimilate **2**
***asir** *(tr)*	grasp, grab, seize, snatch **18**
asistir *(tr)*	assist **4**
asistir a *(tr/intr)*	witness; be present at **4**
asociarse *(refl)*	associate, band together **2**
asociarse con *(refl)*	team up with
asolar *(tr)*	devastate **2**
asomar(se) *(tr/refl)*	lean out, stick out **2**
asombrar *(tr)*	amaze, surprise **2**
asombrarse *(refl)*	wonder **2**
aspirar *(intr)*	inhale **2**
aspirar a *(intr)*	aspire, aim **2**
astillar *(tr)*	splinter, chip **2**
asumir *(tr)*	assume **4**
asustar *(tr)*	frighten, terrify, scare **2**
asustarse *(refl)*	start, startle **2**
atacar *(tr)*	attack, charge **5**
atajar *(tr/intr)*	intercept, cut across **2**
atar *(tr)*	tie, tie up, bundle up **2**
atar con una cuerda *(tr)*	rope together
atender *(tr)*	care for, nurse, look after, tend, treat (*medically*) **19**
atenerse a *(refl)*	abide by, adhere to **54**
aterrar *(tr)*	terrify **2**
aterrizar *(intr)*	land **6**
aterrorizar *(tr)*	terrify, terrorize **6**
atiborrarse de comida *(refl)*	stuff (oneself with food), overeat **2**
atiesar(se) *(tr/refl)*	harden, stiffen, tighten **2**
atomizar *(tr)*	atomize **6**
atormentar *(tr)*	torture **2**
atornillar *(tr)*	screw **2**
atracar *(tr/intr)*	moor, tie up (*nautical*) **5**
atraer *(tr)*	attract, lure **55**
atragantarse *(refl)*	choke **2**
atrancar *(tr)*	bar, bolt (*door*) **5**
atrapar *(tr)*	trap **2**
atravesar *(tr/intr)*	cross, go across; shoot (*rapids*) **19**
atreverse a *(refl)*	dare **3**

	atropellar *(tr)*	knock over, run down, run over **2**
	auditar *(tr)*	audit **2**
	aullar *(intr)*	howl **2**
	aumentar *(tr/intr)*	add to, increase, raise, lift, rise **2**
	aumentarse *(refl)*	increase, enlarge **2**
	ausentarse de *(refl)*	be absent, play truant, absent oneself **2**
	automatizar *(tr)*	automate **2**
	autorizar *(tr)*	authorize, entitle **2**
	avanzar *(tr/intr)*	advance, move forward **6**
	avanzar echando vapor *(intr)*	steam
	aventajar *(tr)*	top, surpass **2**
	aventajar a uno en una vuelta entera *(tr)*	lap
	aventurar *(tr)*	gamble, venture **2**
	avergonzar(se) *(tr/refl)*	shame, be ashamed **6**
	averiarse *(refl)*	get damaged; break down **14**
	***averiguar** *(tr)*	know, find out **8**
	avisar *(tr)*	inform, warn, alert **2**
	avistar *(tr)*	sight **2**
	ayudar *(tr)*	aid, help **2**
	ayunar *(intr)*	fast **2**
	azorar *(tr)*	disturb, upset, embarrass **2**
	azotar *(tr)*	whip **2**
	azucarar *(tr)*	sweeten, sugar **2**
B	**babear** *(intr)*	dribble **2**
	bailar *(intr)*	dance **2**
	bajar *(tr)*	let down, lower, pull down, take down **2**
	bajar *(intr)*	come down, go down, get down, descend; decline, lessen; ebb (*tide*), subside (*water*) **2**
	bajar de *(intr)*	get out of, get off, alight
	balancear(se) *(tr/refl)*	sway, swing, rock **2**
	balar *(intr)*	bleat **2**
	balbucear *(tr/intr)*	stammer, stutter **2**
	bambolearse *(intr)*	totter, sway **2**
	banquetear *(tr/intr)*	feast **2**
	bañar *(tr)*	bath, bathe, dip **2**

	bañarse *(refl)*	bath, take a bath, bathe **2**
	barrear *(tr)*	barricade **2**
	barrer *(tr)*	sweep **3**
	basar en *(tr)*	base on **2**
	bastar *(intr)*	suffice, do, be enough **2**
	batir *(tr)*	beat, hammer **4**
	bautizar *(tr)*	baptise **6**
	beber *(tr)*	drink **3**
	***bendecir** *(tr)*	bless **28**
	beneficiar *(tr)*	benefit, do good to **2**
	besar *(tr)*	kiss **2**
	bifurcarse *(intr)*	fork **5**
	biodegradar(se) *(tr/refl)*	biodegrade **2**
	bizquear *(intr)*	squint **2**
	blandir *(tr)*	wield, flourish, brandish **4**
	blanquear(se) *(tr/refl)*	bleach, whiten **2**
	blasfemar *(intr)*	blaspheme, curse **2**
	bloquear *(tr)*	stop, block; trap **2**
	boicotear *(tr)*	boycott **2**
	bombardear *(tr)*	bomb, shell, bombard **2**
	bombear *(tr)*	pump **2**
	bombearse *(refl)*	warp, bulge **2**
	borbotar *(intr)*	bubble, boil over **2**
	bordar *(tr)*	embroider **2**
	borrar *(tr)*	erase, rub out, scrub, wipe out; write off (*insurance*, *debt*) **2**
	bostezar *(intr)*	yawn **6**
	boxear *(intr)*	box **2**
	bramar *(intr)*	bellow, roar **2**
	brasear *(tr)*	braise **2**
	brillar *(tr/intr)*	glow, gleam, shine **2**
	brincar *(intr)*	hop, skip **5**
	brindar *(tr)*	toast (*with drink*) **2**
	bromear *(intr)*	joke **2**
	broncear(se) *(tr/refl)*	tan **2**
	brotar *(intr)*	spring (from), sprout (from), well up **2**
	burbujear *(intr)*	bubble **2**
	burlar *(tr)*	deceive, circumvent **2**
	buscar *(tr)*	fetch, bring, look for, look up, search, seek **5**
C	**cabalgar** *(tr/intr)*	ride **7**
	cabecear *(intr)*	nod (sleepily), shake one's head **2**

cegar *(tr)*	blind **7, 19**
celebrar *(tr)*	celebrate **2**
cenar *(tr/intr)*	have supper, dine **2**
censurar *(tr)*	censor, censure, reproach **2**
centellear *(intr)*	sparkle **2**
centralizar *(tr)*	centralize **6**
centrifugar *(tr)*	spin **7**
ceñir *(tr)*	surround, skirt **17**
cepillar *(tr)*	brush **2**
cercar *(tr)*	circle, close in, enclose, surround, fence (in) **5**
cercar con un seto *(tr)*	hedge
cerrar(se) *(tr/refl)*	shut, close; turn off (*faucet*) **19**
cerrar con llave *(tr)*	lock
cerrar la cremallera *(tr)*	zip up
cerrar(se) de golpe *(tr/refl)*	slam
cerrar *(intr)*	set in (e.g. *weather*) **19**
certificar *(tr)*	certify **5**
cesar *(intr)*	stop **2**
chantajear *(tr)*	blackmail **2**
chapotear *(intr)*	splash about, paddle (*feet*) **2**
charlar *(intr)*	talk, chat **2**
chasquear *(intr)*	crack, creak (*wood*) **2**
chillar *(intr)*	howl, scream, squeal **2**
chirriar *(intr)*	creak, squeal **2**
chispear *(intr)*	sparkle **2**
chocar *(tr)*	shock **5**
chocar con *(tr)*	hit, crash into, run into, crash
chocar contra *(tr)*	smash into, knock against, bump into
chupar *(tr)*	suck **2**
chutar *(tr)*	shoot (*soccer*) **2**
circular *(tr)*	circulate **2**
citar a *(tr)*	quote, date **2**
citarse con *(refl)*	make an appointment with **2**
clasificar(se) *(tr/refl)*	file, classify, grade, put in order, sort, stream, rank, order, rate **5**
clausurar *(tr)*	close down **2**
clavar *(tr)*	nail, drive in (*nail*), nail down, stick, fix **2**
cobrar *(tr)*	cash; get (*money*); charge (*price*) **2**

cocer *(tr)*	bake, cook **9, 20**
cocer a fuego lento *(tr/intr)*	simmer
cocer al vapor *(tr)*	steam
cocinar *(tr)*	cook **2**
codiciar *(tr)*	lust for/after, covet **2**
coexistir *(intr)*	coexist **4**
***coger** *(tr)*	take, catch, capture, hold; pick, pick up **11**
cohabitar *(intr)*	cohabit **2**
coincidir *(intr)*	coincide **4**
cojear *(intr)*	limp **2**
colaborar *(intr)*	collaborate, cooperate **2**
colar *(tr)*	sieve, sift, strain (*drain water off*) **20**
colegir *(tr)*	collect **11**
colgar *(tr/intr)*	hang, hang up, ring off (*telephone*) **7, 20**
colmar *(tr)*	fill up **2**
colocar *(tr)*	fit, place **5**
colorear *(tr)*	color in **2**
combatir *(tr)*	combat, fight **4**
combinar(se) *(tr/refl)*	combine **2**
comentar *(tr/intr)*	remark, comment **2**
comenzar *(tr/intr)*	start, get started, begin **6, 19**
***comer** *(tr/intr)*	eat, have (to eat) **3**
comer algo *(tr)*	have a snack
comercializar *(tr)*	market, commercialize **6**
comerciar *(tr/intr)*	deal, trade **2**
cometer *(tr)*	commit **3**
comisionar *(tr)*	commission **2**
compadecer(se) de *(tr/refl)*	pity, sympathize, take pity on **32**
comparar *(tr)*	compare **2**
compartir *(tr)*	share **4**
compensar *(tr)*	compensate **2**
competir *(intr)*	compete; race **24**
compilar *(tr)*	compile **2**
completar *(tr)*	complete **2**
complicar *(tr)*	complicate **5**
componer *(tr)*	compose; fix **47**
componerse de *(refl)*	consist (of), comprise **47**
comportarse *(refl)*	behave **2**
***comprar** *(tr)*	buy, purchase; take over (*business*) **2**
comprender *(tr)*	comprise, understand **2**

comprimir *(tr)*	compress **4**
comprobar *(tr)*	check, prove, check up, verify **20**
comprometerse a *(refl)*	commit oneself to **3**
computar *(tr)*	compute **2**
comulgar *(tr/intr)*	give, take communion **7**
comunicar *(tr/intr)*	communicate, convey **5**
concebir *(tr)*	conceive **4**
conceder *(tr)*	allow, award (*prize*), concede, cede; confer, grant **3**
concentrarse en *(refl)*	concentrate, gather, concentrate on, center on **2**
concernir *(tr)*	concern **19**
concluir *(tr/intr)*	accomplish, conclude, close (*sale*), finish **12**
concordar con *(intr)*	accord with **20**
condenar *(tr)*	condemn, convict, damn, curse, sentence **2**
condensar *(tr)*	condense **2**
condimentar con *(tr)*	condiment, flavor, season **2**
condolerse *(refl)*	sympathize **20**
***conducir** *(tr)*	conduct, drive, lead, guide **31**
conducirse *(refl)*	behave **31**
conectar *(tr)*	connect, switch on, turn on **2**
confeccionar *(tr)*	make out (*list*); tailor **2**
conferenciar *(intr)*	confer, be in conference **2**
confesar *(tr)*	confess **19**
confiar en *(tr/intr)*	confide, entrust, trust, confide in **14**
confinar con *(tr)*	confine, border on **2**
confirmar *(tr)*	confirm, endorse **2**
confiscar *(tr)*	confiscate **5**
conformarse a *(refl)*	conform to **2**
conformarse con *(refl)*	comply with **2**
confortar *(tr)*	comfort **2**
confrontar *(tr)*	confront **2**
confundir *(tr)*	confuse, bewilder, muddle up, puzzle **4**
congelar(se) *(tr/refl)*	gather, flock together, congregate, crowd **7**
conjurar *(intr)*	conjure **2**
conmemorar *(tr)*	commemorate **2**

contribuir *(tr)*	contribute **12**
controlar *(tr)*	check, inspect, monitor, control **2**
contundir *(tr)*	bruise **4**
convencer *(tr)*	convince, bring around **9**
convenir en *(tr)*	fit, suit, agree to, arrive at **57**
conversar con *(intr)*	converse with, speak **2**
convertir *(tr)*	transform, convert **22**
convertirse en *(refl)*	turn, change, turn into **22**
convidar *(tr)*	invite, treat **2**
convivir *(intr)*	coexist **4**
convocar *(tr)*	summon, call a meeting **5**
cooperar *(intr)*	cooperate **2**
coordinar *(tr)*	coordinate **2**
copiar *(tr)*	copy, reproduce, transcribe, write out **2**
coquetear *(intr)*	flirt **2**
coronar *(tr)*	crown, cap **2**
corregir *(tr)*	correct, edit **11, 24**
correr *(intr)*	run, flow, race, slip, stream **3**
corresponder a *(intr)*	correspond (to), write **3**
corroer(se) *(tr/refl)*	corrode, erode, rust **30**
corromper(se) *(tr/refl)*	rot, decay, corrupt **3**
cortar *(tr/intr)*	cut, chop, clip, mow, slice, trim, cut off, cut out, cut up, crop; excise, incise; turn off, switch off; turn out; break in (*conversation*) **2**
cortejar *(tr)*	court, woo **2**
cosechar *(tr)*	harvest, reap **2**
coser *(tr)*	sew, stitch **3**
cosquillear *(tr)*	tickle **2**
costar *(tr)*	cost **20**
cotizar *(tr)*	quote, price, value **6**
crear *(tr)*	create **2**
crecer *(intr)*	grow **32**
creer *(tr)*	think, believe **13**
crepitar *(intr)*	crackle, sizzle **2**
criar *(tr)*	bring up (*children*) **14**
cristalizar *(tr)*	crystallize **6**
criticar *(tr)*	criticize **5**
croar *(intr)*	croak **2**
cronometrar *(tr)*	time **2**
crucificar *(tr)*	crucify **5**

darse prisa *(refl)*	hurry, hurry up, rush
datar de *(intr)*	date from **2**
deambular *(intr)*	saunter **2**
debatir *(tr)*	debate, discuss **4**
deber *(tr)*	owe **3**
deber *(intr)*	have to, must, ought, should, be supposed to **3**
deber de *(intr)*	must, ought (*probability*)
debilitar(se) *(tr/refl)*	weaken; wilt **2**
decaer *(intr)*	decay, decline **30**
decepcionar *(tr)*	disappoint **2**
decidir *(tr)*	decide **4**
decidir por *(tr)*	decide on
decidirse *(refl)*	make up one's mind **4**
***decir** *(tr/intr)*	say, tell **34**
declarar *(tr/intr)*	declare, allege, state **2**
decorar *(tr)*	decorate **2**
decretar *(tr)*	decree **2**
dedicar *(tr)*	dedicate **5**
dedicar(se) a *(tr/refl)*	take up, dedicate (oneself) to, devote (oneself) to **5**
deducir *(tr)*	deduce **31**
defender *(tr)*	defend, champion, stand up for, guard **19**
definir *(tr)*	define **4**
deformar *(tr)*	deform **2**
defraudar *(tr)*	cheat, defraud, cheat, deceive **2**
degradar *(tr)*	degrade **2**
dejar *(tr)*	leave, let, desert **2**
dejar caer *(tr)*	drop, let fall
dejar de lado *(tr)*	put aside
dejar de *(intr)*	fail (to do), stop (. . .ing)
dejar entrar *(tr)*	let in
dejar pasar *(tr)*	let by/through
dejar perplejo *(tr)*	bewilder
dejar sin sentido a *(tr)*	knock out
dejarse caer *(refl)*	flop down **2**
delegar *(tr)*	delegate **7**
deleitar *(tr)*	delight **2**
deletrear *(tr)*	spell, spell out **2**
delirar *(intr)*	rave **2**
demorar(se) *(tr/refl)*	delay **2**
demostrar *(tr)*	demonstrate, prove, show **20**
denominar *(tr)*	name, term **2**

	take down **7, 20**
descolorar *(intr)*	fade **2**
descomponer(se) *(tr/refl)*	break down, disperse, decompose, rot **47**
desconcertar *(tr)*	embarrass, throw off balance **19**
desconectar *(tr)*	disconnect, switch off, turn off **2**
desconfiar de *(tr)*	distrust **14**
descongelar *(tr)*	defrost, thaw, de-ice **2**
descontar *(tr)*	deduct, discount **20**
describir *(tr)*	describe **37**
descubrir *(tr)*	discover, find out, strike (*oil*), uncover, bare **25**
descuidar *(tr)*	neglect **2**
desdecir(se) *(tr/refl)*	withdraw; clash **34**
desdeñar *(tr)*	scorn **2**
desear *(tr)*	desire, want, wish, wish for **2**
desechar *(tr)*	throw away **2**
desembalar *(tr)*	unpack **2**
desembarazarse de *(refl)*	rid, rid oneself of **6**
desembarcar *(intr)*	disembark, land **5**
desembocar en *(intr)*	flow into **5**
desembolsar *(tr)*	pay out **2**
desempolvar *(tr)*	dust **2**
desenganchar *(tr)*	unhook, uncouple **2**
desenredar *(tr)*	disentangle **2**
desenterrar *(tr)*	dig up, unearth **19**
desenvainar *(tr)*	shell (*peas*) **2**
desertar *(tr)*	desert **19**
desesperar *(intr)*	despair **2**
desfigurar *(tr)*	disfigure, deface **2**
desgarrar *(tr)*	tear **2**
desguazar *(tr)*	scrap **2**
deshacer *(tr)*	break up, ruin; undo, unpack (*suitcase*) **41**
deshacerse de *(refl)*	dispense with, dump, get rid of
deshelar *(tr)*	defrost, de-ice **19**
deshelar(se) *(tr/refl)*	thaw
desherbar *(tr)*	weed **19**
desheredar *(tr)*	disinherit **2**
deshollinar *(tr)*	sweep (*chimney*) **2**
designar *(tr)*	name, designate **2**
desilusionar *(tr)*	disappoint **2**
desinfectar *(tr)*	disinfect **2**

desinflar *(tr)*	deflate **2**
desintegrar(se) *(intr/refl)*	disintegrate **2**
deslizarse *(intr)*	creep, glide, steal, move stealthily, slip, slide **6**
deslumbrar *(tr)*	dazzle **2**
desmaquillarse *(refl)*	remove make-up **2**
desmayar *(intr)*	faint **2**
desmentir *(tr)*	contradict **22**
desmenuzar(se) *(intr/refl)*	crumble; cut up **6**
desmigajar(se) *(tr/refl)*	crumble **2**
desmontar *(tr)*	take down, dismantle (e.g. *tent*) **2**
desmoronarse *(refl)*	decay, decline **2**
desnudar(se) *(tr/refl)*	bare, strip off, undress, get undressed **2**
desobedecer *(tr/intr)*	disobey **32**
desobstruir *(tr)*	unblock **12**
desoír *(tr)*	ignore, turn a deaf ear to **44**
desollar *(tr)*	skin **20**
desorganizar *(tr)*	disorganize **6**
despachar *(tr)*	despatch, dispatch, send off **2**
desparramarse *(refl)*	scatter **2**
despedir *(tr)*	dismiss, fire/sack **24**
despedir(se) *(tr/refl)*	take leave of, say goodbye to, see off **24**
despegar *(tr/intr)*	lift off (*rocket*), take off, blast off; take down (e.g. *poster*), detach, unstick **7**
despejar(se) *(tr/refl)*	clear, clear up, brighten up **2**
despellejar *(tr)*	skin **2**
despertar(se) *(tr/refl)*	awaken, arouse, wake, wake up **19**
despilfarrar *(tr)*	waste **2**
desplazar *(tr)*	displace **6**
desplazar hacia arriba *(intr)*	scroll up
desplazar hacia abajo *(intr)*	scroll down
desplegar *(tr)*	display (*computing*) **7, 19**
despojar(se) de *(tr/refl)*	take off, shed **2**
despreciar *(tr)*	scorn **2**
destacar(se) *(tr/refl)*	show up, stand out, be noticeable, highlight; star **5**

destapar *(tr)*	uncover **2**
destellar *(intr)*	sparkle, flash, sparkle **2**
desterrar *(tr)*	banish, exile **19**
destilar *(tr)*	distil **2**
destornillar *(tr)*	unscrew **2**
destruir *(tr)*	destroy, wreck **12**
desvalorizar *(tr)*	devalue **6**
desviar *(intr)*	switch (*change direction*), divert **14**
desviar(se) de *(refl)*	deviate, detour, skew **14**
detallar *(tr)*	detail **2**
detectar *(tr)*	detect **2**
detener(se) *(tr/refl)*	detain, arrest; stem, stop **54**
deteriorar *(intr)*	decay, deteriorate **2**
determinar *(tr)*	determine **2**
detestar *(tr)*	detest, hate **2**
devaluar *(tr)*	devalue **15**
devastar *(tr)*	devastate **2**
devolver *(tr)*	give back, hand back, pay back; return, send back, take back (*goods*) **20**
devolver a su sitio *(tr)*	replace
devolverse *(refl)*	turn over **20**
devorar *(tr)*	devour **2**
diagnosticar *(tr)*	diagnose **5**
dibujar *(tr)*	draw, sketch in **2**
dictar *(tr)*	dictate **2**
difamar *(tr)*	slander **2**
diferenciar *(tr)*	differentiate **2**
diferenciarse de *(refl)*	differ **2**
diferir *(intr)*	differ **22**
dificultar *(tr)*	hinder **2**
difundir *(tr)*	spread, diffuse **4**
digerir *(tr)*	digest **22**
dignarse *(refl)*	deign to **2**
diluir *(tr)*	dilute **12**
dimitir *(tr)*	resign **4**
diputar *(tr)*	deputize, delegate **2**
dirigir *(tr)*	address (e.g. *letter*); direct, manage, steer **11**
dirigirse a/hacia *(refl)*	accost, address (*a person*); make for, head for, make one's way **11**
discernir *(tr)*	discern **19**

disciplinar *(tr)*	discipline **2**
disculpar *(tr)*	excuse, exonerate, forgive **2**
disculparse de *(refl)*	apologize for, say sorry, regret **2**
discutir *(tr/intr)*	discuss, argue, speak, debate **4**
diseminar *(tr)*	spread, disseminate **2**
diseñar *(tr)*	design, style **2**
disfrazar *(tr)*	disguise **6**
disfrutar de *(tr)*	enjoy **2**
disgregarse *(refl)*	disintegrate **7**
disimular *(tr)*	conceal; pretend **2**
dislocarse *(refl)*	pull a muscle, dislocate **5**
disminuir *(tr/intr)*	diminish, decline, decrease, lessen, dwindle, shrink, slacken **12**
disolver(se) *(tr/refl)*	dissolve **20**
disparar *(tr/intr)*	fire, discharge, shoot **2**
dispensar de *(tr)*	exempt from, pardon **2**
dispersar(se) *(tr/refl)*	scatter, disperse **2**
disponer de *(tr)*	dispose of; have available, spare (*time*) **47**
disputar *(tr/intr)*	argue, quarrel, dispute **2**
***distinguir (de)** *(tr)*	distinguish, differentiate, make out **10**
distinguir entre *(tr)*	tell (apart)
distinguirse *(refl)*	shine, excel **10**
distraer *(tr)*	distract **55**
distribuir *(tr)*	give out, distribute, share out **12**
disuadir *(tr)*	dissuade **4**
divagar *(intr)*	ramble on, waffle **7**
divertir *(tr)*	amuse, divert, entertain **22**
divertirse *(refl)*	enjoy oneself, have a good time, have fun, play around, play about **22**
dividir *(tr)*	divide, cut up **4**
divisar *(tr)*	make out, sight, spy, espy **2**
divorciar(se) *(tr/refl)*	divorce, get divorced **2**
divulgar *(tr)*	spread, divulge **2**
doblar(se) *(tr/refl)*	double; turn back, fold, fold up; bend down, bend over **2**

doler *(tr/intr)*	ache, hurt, distress, pain **20**
domar *(tr)*	tame **2**
domesticar *(tr)*	tame **5**
dominar *(tr)*	boss about; master (*a subject*); overlook, look out over **2**
dominarse *(refl)*	control oneself **2**
donar *(tr)*	donate **2**
***dormir** *(intr)*	sleep **23**
dormirse *(refl)*	fall asleep, go to sleep, doze off, drop off **23**
drogar *(tr)*	drug, dope **7**
drogarse *(refl)*	take drugs
duchar(se) *(tr/refl)*	shower **2**
dudar *(tr)*	doubt **2**
duplicar *(tr)*	double; duplicate **5**
durar *(tr/intr)*	hold out, last, go on, last; take (*time*) **2**

E

echar *(tr)*	pour; sprout; throw, cast, toss, throw away **2**
echar a correos/al correo *(tr)*	mail, post
echar de menos a *(tr)*	miss (somebody)
echar la culpa a *(tr)*	blame
echar un vistazo *(intr)*	glance
echar vapor *(intr)*	steam
echarse *(refl)*	lie (down) **2**
echarse atrás *(refl)*	back down
economizar *(tr)*	economize **6**
editar *(tr)*	edit **2**
educar *(tr)*	educate, bring up **5**
efectuar *(tr)*	bring about **15**
ejecutar *(tr)*	execute, realize; carry out; run (*computing*) **2**
ejercer *(tr)*	exercise **9**
ejercitarse *(refl)*	exercise **2**
elaborar *(tr)*	brew, think out, work out (*plan*) **2**
electrificar *(tr)*	electrify **5**
elegir *(tr)*	choose, elect, select, pick; vote **11, 24**
elevar *(tr)*	elevate, heighten **2**
eliminar *(tr)*	eliminate, do away with, excise, get rid of **2**
elogiar *(tr)*	praise **2**

enclavijar *(tr)*	peg **2**
encoger(se) *(tr/refl)*	cower, flinch, shrink **11**
encogerse de hombros *(refl)*	shrug
encontrar(se) *(tr/refl)*	find, meet, run into **20**
encorvar(se) *(tr/refl)*	stoop, bend over; curve **2**
enderezar(se) *(tr/refl)*	straighten **6**
endosar *(tr)*	endorse **2**
endulzar *(tr)*	sweeten **6**
endurecer(se) *(tr/refl)*	harden, stiffen **32**
enfadar(se) *(tr/refl)*	anger, annoy; get annoyed **2**
enfermar(se) *(intr/refl)*	become sick, fall ill **2**
enfrascar *(tr)*	bottle **5**
enfrentarse con *(refl)*	confront, face up to **2**
enfriar *(tr)*	cool down **14**
enfurecer *(tr)*	madden **32**
enganchar *(tr)*	hook, hook up; harness (*horse to a cart*) **2**
engañar *(tr)*	deceive, fool, bluff, trick **2**
engordar *(tr/intr)*	fatten **2**
engrasar *(tr)*	grease **2**
engullir *(tr)*	guzzle, swallow **16**
enhebrar *(tr)*	thread **19**
enjabonar *(tr)*	soap **2**
enjaezar *(tr)*	harness **6**
enjuagar *(tr)*	rinse **7**
enjugar *(tr)*	wipe, dry **2, 21**
enlazar *(tr)*	bind, tie, tie up **6**
enlazar con *(intr)*	liaise with
enlazar con *(tr)*	connect with/up to, link with
enloquecer *(tr)*	madden **32**
enlucir *(tr)*	plaster **43**
enmarcar *(tr)*	frame **5**
enmendar *(tr)*	amend **19**
enmohecer(se)	go moldy **32**
ennegrecer(se) *(tr/refl)*	blacken **32**
enojar(se) *(tr/refl)*	annoy, anger, get angry, lose one's temper, get annoyed **2**
enriquecer *(tr)*	enrich **32**
enrollar *(tr/intr)*	coil, roll open **2**
ensanchar *(tr)*	widen, broaden, extend, enlarge **2**
ensartar *(tr)*	string (together), thread **2**
ensayar *(tr)*	rehearse, try, try out **2**

esbozar *(tr)*	sketch out **6**
escabullirse *(refl)*	slip away, break off **16**
escalar *(tr)*	climb, scale **2**
escapar(se) *(refl)*	run away, escape **2**
escardar *(tr)*	weed **2**
esclarecer *(intr)*	clear up **32**
esclavizar *(tr)*	enslave **6**
escocer *(tr)*	upset; sting **9, 20**
escoger *(tr)*	choose, select **11**
esconder(se) *(tr/refl)*	hide **3**
***escribir** *(tr)*	write, write in, write out, write up **37**
escribir a máquina *(tr)*	type
escribir solicitando algo *(intr)*	write away/off for something
escuchar *(tr)*	listen **2**
escuchar clandestinamente *(tr)*	bug **2**
escudriñar *(tr)*	check over, search **2**
escupir *(intr)*	spit **4**
escurrir *(tr)*	wring **4**
esforzarse (por) *(refl)*	make an effort, strain, struggle, try **6, 20**
esgrimir *(intr)*	fence (*sport*) **4**
esnifar *(tr)*	sniff **2**
espabilar la borrachera *(intr)*	sober up **2**
espantar *(tr)*	scare, frighten **2**
esparcir *(tr)*	scatter; sow **9**
especificar *(tr)*	specify **5**
especializar *(intr)*	specialize **6**
especular *(tr/intr)*	speculate, gamble **2**
esperar *(tr/intr)*	wait, await; hope; expect **2**
espesar(se) *(tr/refl)*	thicken **2**
espiar *(intr)*	spy **14**
espumar *(intr)*	foam **2**
esquiar *(intr)*	ski **2**
esquilar *(tr)*	shear, clip **2**
estabilizar(se) *(tr/refl)*	stabilize, steady **6**
establecer *(tr)*	establish, found, set up **32**
establecerse *(refl)*	settle **32**
establecerse sin derecho *(refl)*	squat
estacionar *(tr)*	park; garage **2**
estafar *(tr)*	deceive, cheat, take in, trick **2**
estallar *(intr)*	explode, go bang, blow up **2**

estornudar *(intr)*	sneeze **2**
estrangular *(tr)*	strangle, throttle **2**
estrechar(se) *(tr/refl)*	extend, hold out; narrow; tighten; shake (hands) **2**
estrellar *(intr)*	crash **2**
estremecerse *(refl)*	quiver, shiver, shudder, tremble **32**
estrenar *(tr)*	release (*film*, etc.); open (*show*); wear for the first time **2**
estropear *(tr)*	ruin, spoil, harm **2**
estructurar *(tr)*	structure **2**
estudiar *(tr/intr)*	study, do (*subject*) **2**
etiquetar *(tr)*	label **2**
evacuar *(tr)*	evacuate **2**
evadir(se) *(tr/refl)*	run away, dodge, evade **2**
evaluar *(tr)*	evaluate, appraise **2**
evitar *(tr)*	avoid **2**
evocar *(tr)*	evoke **5**
evolucionar *(tr)*	evolve **2**
exagerar *(tr)*	exaggerate **2**
examinar *(tr)*	examine, check, study, search, test, view **2**
exasperar *(tr)*	exasperate **2**
excavar *(tr)*	dig, hollow out **2**
exceder *(tr)*	exceed, top, surpass **3**
exceder la velocidad permitida *(intr)*	speed
exceptuar *(tr)*	except **15**
excitar *(tr)*	excite, cause, work up (*interest*, *emotion*, etc.) **2**
exclamar *(tr)*	exclaim **2**
excluir (de) *(tr)*	exclude (from) **12**
exculpar *(tr)*	exonerate **2**
exhalar *(tr)*	exhale **2**
exhibir *(tr)*	exhibit **4**
exigir *(tr)*	claim, demand; require, want **11**
existir *(intr)*	exist **4**
expedir *(tr)*	dispatch, send off **24**
experimentar *(tr)*	experience, feel; experiment **2**
explrar *(tr)*	expire **2**
explicar *(tr)*	explain, give reasons **5**
explorar *(tr)*	explore **2**

	explosionar *(intr)*	explode, blow up **2**
	explotar *(tr/intr)*	explode, blow up, set off (*explosion*) **2**
	exponer *(tr)*	expose, display **47**
	exportar *(tr)*	export **2**
	expresar *(tr)*	express; quote **2**
	exprimir *(tr)*	squeeze (out), wring **4**
	extender(se) *(tr/refl)*	stretch, extend, spread, spread out; widen, enlarge, expand; lay out **19**
	extender la mano	reach (out for)
	extinguir *(tr)*	extinguish **10**
	extraer *(tr)*	extract **55**
	extraer minerales *(tr)*	mine
	extrañar *(tr)*	surprise **2**
	extraviarse *(refl)*	stray **14**
F	**fabricar** *(tr)*	make, manufacture **5**
	facilitar *(tr)*	facilitate; supply, provide **2**
	facturar *(tr)*	bill; check in (*baggage*) **2**
	fallar *(intr)*	fail, miss **2**
	falsificar *(tr)*	fake **5**
	faltar *(intr)*	lack, be missing; fail, let down **2**
	fascinar *(tr)*	fascinate **2**
	fastidiar *(tr)*	mess (someone) about, get on someone's nerves, tease **2**
	fatigar(se) *(tr/refl)*	tire **7**
	favorecer *(tr)*	favor **32**
	faxear *(tr)*	fax **2**
	felicitar *(tr)*	congratulate; compliment **2**
	fermentar *(tr/intr)*	ferment **2**
	festejar *(tr)*	feast, celebrate, fete **2**
	fiarse de *(refl)*	trust **14**
	fichar *(tr)*	file; index **2**
	fichar (la entrada) *(intr)*	clock in
	fichar (la salida) *(intr)*	clock out
	fijar *(tr)*	fix, fasten, secure **2**
	filmar *(tr)*	film, shoot (*film*) **2**
	filtrar(se) *(tr/refl)*	filter, seep **2**
	financiar *(tr)*	finance **2**
	fingir *(tr/intr)*	pretend, fake, feign **11**

	firmar *(tr)*	sign **2**
	firmar el registro	book in
	fletar *(tr)*	charter (*plane*, *boat*) **2**
	flirtear *(intr)*	flirt **2**
	florecer *(intr)*	flourish, flower, bloom, come out **32**
	flotar *(intr)*	float, hover **2**
	fluir *(intr)*	flow, stream **12**
	fondear *(intr)*	anchor **2**
	forjar *(tr)*	form, fashion **2**
	formar *(tr)*	form, fashion, shape, train **2**
	formatear *(tr)*	format (*computing*) **2**
	fortalecer *(tr)*	strengthen, reinforce **32**
	forzar *(tr)*	force, compel; rape **6, 20**
	forzar una entrada *(intr)*	break in **6**
	fotocopiar *(tr)*	(photo)copy, duplicate **2**
	fotografiar *(tr)*	photograph, shoot **14**
	fracasar *(intr)*	crash **2**
	fracturar(se) *(tr/intr)*	fracture **2**
	franquear *(tr)*	frank **2**
	frecuentar *(tr)*	frequent **2**
	fregar *(tr)*	scrub, wash up **7, 19**
	***freír(se)** *(tr/refl)*	fry **39**
	frenar *(intr)*	brake **2**
	friccionar *(tr)*	rub **2**
	frotar *(tr)*	rub **2**
	fruncir(se) *(tr/refl)*	wrinkle **9**
	frustrar *(tr)*	frustrate, foil, thwart **2**
	fugarse *(intr)*	flee **7**
	fumar *(tr/intr)*	smoke **2**
	funcionar *(intr)*	work, function; act, behave **2**
	fundar *(tr)*	found **2**
	fundir(se) *(tr/refl)*	fuse, melt, blow (*fuse*) **4**
	fusionar *(tr)*	merge **2**
	fusionar(se) *(tr/refl)*	fuse **2**
G	**ganar** *(tr/intr)*	earn; win **2**
	gandulear *(intr)*	idle about **2**
	garantizar *(tr)*	guarantee, secure **6**
	garrapatear *(intr)*	scribble **2**
	gastar *(tr)*	spend (*money*); use up **2**
	gemir *(intr)*	groan, moan **24**
	generar *(tr)*	generate **2**

	Verb	Meaning / model
	girar *(tr/intr)*	turn, gyrate, orbit, spin, wheel **2**
	girar hacia adelante *(tr)*	wind on, forward
	girar hacia atrás *(tr)*	wind back
	gobernar *(tr/intr)*	govern; steer (*ship*) **19**
	golpear *(tr)*	hit, bash, beat, slap, smack, knock, tap, strike **2**
	gorjear *(intr)*	sing (*birds*), twitter **2**
	gotear *(intr)*	drip, trickle **2**
	gozar *(tr)*	enjoy **6**
	gozar de boom *(intr)*	boom
	grabar *(tr)*	engrave; record, tape; save (*computing*) **2**
	graduarse *(refl)*	qualify, graduate **15**
	granizar *(intr)*	hail (stones) **6**
	grapar *(tr)*	staple **2**
	graznar *(intr)*	croak, squawk **2**
	gritar *(tr/intr)*	shout, call out, cry (out) **2**
	***gruñir** *(intr)*	growl, grunt **17**
	guardar *(tr)*	guard, watch (over); keep, store, put away (safely); hold, keep back; save (*computing*) **2**
	guiar *(tr)*	guide, steer **14**
	guiñar *(tr)*	blink; wink **2**
	gustar *(tr)*	please (used for *like*) **2**
H	***haber** *(intr)*	have (auxiliary) **40**
	hablar *(tr/intr)*	talk, speak (*language*) **2**
	hablar claro *(intr)*	speak out
	hablar mal de *(tr)*	speak ill of
	***hacer** *(tr)*	do, make, get someone to do something **41**
	hacer a multicopista *(tr)*	duplicate
	hacer abandonar una costumbre *(tr)*	break someone of a habit
	hacer aparecer *(tr)*	conjure up
	hacer autostop *(intr)*	hitch-hike
	hacer bricolaje *(intr)*	do odd jobs, do DIY
	hacer callar *(tr)*	silence
	hacer camping *(intr)*	camp
	hacer circular *(tr)*	circulate
	hacer cola *(intr)*	get in line, queue
	hacer compras *(intr)*	shop, go shopping
	hacer constar *(tr)*	minute, take minutes

hacer contrabando *(tr)*	smuggle
hacer correr *(tr)*	race
hacer correspondencia *(intr)*	change (*trains*)
hacer daño a *(tr)*	harm
hacer desaparecer *(tr)*	conjure (*make disappear*)
hacer eco *(intr)*	echo
hacer el amor *(intr)*	make love
hacer estallar *(tr)*	trigger off
hacer falta *(tr)*	be necessary (*need*)
hacer footing *(intr)*	jog
hacer frente a *(tr)*	confront, face up to, stand up to; cope with
hacer funcionar *(tr)*	operate, make work
hacer gala de *(tr)*	show off
hacer gimnasia *(intr)*	do gymnastics
hacer girar *(tr)*	wheel, turn
hacer juegos de manos *(intr)*	conjure
hacer las maletas	pack suitcases
hacer mal a *(tr)*	hurt, damage
hacer pasar *(tr)*	show in
hacer por turnos *(intr)*	take turns
hacer prisionero a *(tr)*	take prisoner
hacer proyectos *(intr)*	plan, make plans
hacer punto *(intr)*	knit
hacer que uno pierda el equilibrio	throw off balance
hacer rodar *(tr)*	roll, wheel
hacer trampas *(intr)*	cheat
hacer trasbordo *(intr)*	change (*trains*)
hacer tropezar *(tr)*	trip
hacer un vídeo de *(tr)*	video
hacer una huelga *(intr)*	strike, go on strike
hacer una pausa *(tr)*	pause
hacerse *(refl)*	become (*prospects, existence*), get, turn, change **41**
hacerse a la vela	sail
hacerse hombre/mujer mayor	grow up
hacer(se) amigos *(tr/refl)*	make friends
hacer(se) borroso *(tr/refl)*	blur, become blurred
hacer(se) más rígido *(tr/refl)*	harden, stiffen
halagar *(tr)*	coax, flatter **7**

importarle a uno	matter; mind
importunar *(tr)*	molest, pester **2**
impresionar *(tr/intr)*	impress; strike **2**
imprimir *(tr)*	print, print out, run off **4**
impulsar *(tr)*	operate; impel **2**
incapacitar *(tr)*	incapacitate, disqualify **2**
incendiar(se) *(tr/refl)*	light, ignite **2**
incinerar *(tr)*	cremate, incinerate **2**
incitar *(tr)*	urge **2**
inclinar(se) *(tr/refl)*	nod, bow; bend, bend over, stoop, lean; slope **2**
incluir *(tr)*	include, count in **12**
incorporar(se) *(tr/refl)*	include, incorporate; join, sit up (*from lying*), get up (*from reclining position*) **2**
indicar *(tr)*	indicate, denote, point (out/to), show **5**
indisponer *(tr)*	indispose **47**
inducir *(tr)*	induce **31**
infectar *(tr)*	infect **2**
inferir *(tr)*	infer **22**
inflar *(tr)*	blow up, inflate, swell **2**
influenciar *(tr)*	influence **2**
influir *(tr)*	influence **12**
informar(se) sobre *(tr/refl)*	inform, inform oneself, get information about **2**
infringir *(tr)*	infringe **11**
ingresar *(tr)*	deposit, pay in, bank **2**
inhalar *(tr/intr)*	inhale, sniff **2**
inicializar *(tr)*	initialize, boot (*computing*) **6**
iniciar *(tr)*	initiate **2**
injertar en *(tr)*	graft onto **2**
injuriar *(tr)*	insult **2**
inmigrar *(intr)*	immigrate **2**
inmovilizar *(tr)*	pin down **6**
inmunizar *(tr)*	immunize **6**
inocular *(tr)*	innoculate **2**
inquietar(se) *(tr/refl)*	worry, disturb **2**
inscribir(se) *(tr/refl)*	enrol **37**
insertar *(tr)*	insert, write in **2**
insinuar *(tr)*	insinuate **15**
insistir *(tr/intr)*	insist **4**

	Spanish	English
	irse *(refl)*	go away, leave, clear off **42**
	irse volando *(refl)*	fly away
	irritar *(tr)*	irritate **2**
J	**jabonar** *(tr)*	soap **2**
	jactarse de *(refl)*	boast (of) **2**
	jadear *(intr)*	gasp, pant **2**
	jubilar(se) *(tr/refl)*	retire **2**
	***jugar (a)** *(intr)*	play; act out, play a part, play around; gamble **21**
	jugar el papel de *(intr)*	act out, play a role
	juntar(se) *(tr/refl)*	join, couple, put together, pool (resources); assemble, unite **2**
	jurar *(tr/intr)*	swear **2**
	justificar *(tr)*	justify **5**
	juzgar *(tr)*	judge, arbitrate; try, prosecute **7**
	juzgar mal *(tr)*	misjudge
L	**labrar** *(tr)*	farm, cultivate, till **2**
	ladear *(tr)*	skirt around; incline **2**
	ladrar *(intr)*	bark **2**
	lamentar *(tr/intr)*	lament, feel sorry, be sorry, regret **2**
	lamer *(tr)*	lick **4**
	languidecer *(intr)*	pine (away) **32**
	lanzar *(tr)*	throw, bowl, cast, launch **6**
	lanzarse *(refl)*	rush, hurry; shoot, move quickly **6**
	largar(se) de *(tr/refl)*	get out of way of, go away, clear off, clear out **7**
	lastimar *(tr)*	hurt, damage **2**
	latir *(intr)*	beat (*heart*) **4**
	***lavar(se)** *(tr/refl)*	wash **1**
	***leer** *(tr/intr)*	read **13**
	leer en voz alta *(tr)*	read aloud
	legalizar *(tr)*	legalize **6**
	legar *(tr)*	leave, bequeath **7**
	legitimar *(tr)*	legalize **2**
	levantar *(tr)*	lift, raise, hoist; erect, rear **2**
	levantar los ojos	look up

	lubricar *(tr)*	grease **5**
	lubrificar *(tr)*	lubricate, oil **5**
	luchar con/contra *(tr/intr)*	fight, struggle, wrestle **2**
	***lucir(se)** *(tr/intr/refl)*	shine, excel, show off **43**
M	**machacar** *(tr)*	mash, pound **5**
	madurar *(tr/intr)*	ripen **2**
	magnetizar *(tr)*	magnetize **6**
	maldecir *(tr)*	curse, damn **28**
	malear(se) *(tr/refl)*	sour **2**
	malgastar *(tr)*	waste **2**
	malinterpretar *(tr)*	misinterpret **2**
	malparir *(intr)*	miscarry **4**
	maltratar *(tr)*	maltreat, mistreat, abuse **2**
	malversar *(tr)*	embezzle **2**
	mamar *(tr)*	suck, suckle **2**
	manar *(intr)*	run, flow, well up **2**
	manchar(se) *(tr/refl)*	soil, spot, stain, mark **2**
	mandar *(tr)*	command, lead; order, tell; send **2**
	mandar por correo *(tr)*	post, mail
	manejar *(tr)*	manage; operate (*machine*); steer, process (*data*, etc.) **2**
	manifestar *(tr)*	declare, state **19**
	manosear *(tr)*	handle **2**
	mantener *(tr)*	keep, maintain, provide for, support **54**
	mantenerse alejado *(refl)*	keep away
	mantener(se) bien *(tr/refl)*	steady, stand firm, stand one's ground, hold on, hold firm, hold up
	maquillar *(tr)*	make up, apply make-up **2**
	marcar *(tr)*	dial; mark; score **5**
	marchar *(intr)*	march; work, function **2**
	marcharse *(intr)*	go away, leave, go off **2**
	marchitar(se) *(tr/intr/refl)*	fade, wither, wilt **2**
	marearse *(refl)*	be seasick; feel sick/dizzy **2**
	marginarse *(refl)*	drop out (*of society*) **2**
	martillar *(tr)*	hammer **2**
	masacrar *(tr)*	massacre **2**

	monopolizar *(tr)*	monopolize **6**
	montar *(tr)*	assemble, erect; mount **2**
	montar (en) *(tr/intr)*	ride
	montar a caballo *(intr)*	go horse riding, hack
	morder *(tr)*	bite **20**
	mordiscar *(tr/intr)*	nibble **5**
	morir *(intr)*	die **23**
	morir de hambre *(intr)*	starve (*to death*)
	mortificar *(tr)*	spite **5**
	mostrar *(tr)*	show **20**
	motivar *(tr)*	motivate **2**
	mover(se) *(tr/refl)*	stir; move; wag **20**
	mudar(se) de *(tr)*	change; moult; move house **2**
	muestrear *(tr)*	sample **2**
	multar *(tr)*	fine **2**
	multiplicar(se) *(tr/refl)*	multiply **5**
	murmullar *(tr/intr)*	murmur **2**
	mutilar *(tr)*	mutilate, disfigure, deface **2**
N	**nacer** *(intr)*	be born **32**
	nadar *(intr)*	swim **2**
	narrar *(tr)*	narrate, relate, report **2**
	naufragar *(tr/intr)*	wreck, be shipwrecked **7**
	navegar *(tr)*	sail, navigate **7**
	necesitar *(tr)*	need, require; want **2**
	negar *(tr)*	deny, disclaim **7, 19**
	negociar con *(tr/intr)*	negotiate; do business with **2**
	neutralizar *(tr)*	neutralize **6**
	nevar *(intr)*	snow **19**
	nombrar *(tr)*	appoint, engage, nominate, commission; name; create **2**
	normalizar *(tr)*	standardize **6**
	notar *(tr)*	note, remark; notice, spot, see **2**
	nublarse *(refl)*	cloud over **2**
	nutrir *(tr)*	feed **4**
O	**obedecer** *(tr)*	obey **32**
	obligar a *(tr)*	force, oblige, compel, constrain **7**
	obrar (de acuerdo con) *(intr)*	act (on) **2**

P

pacer *(tr/intr)*	graze **32**
padecer de *(tr/intr)*	suffer, suffer from **32**
padecer hambre *(intr)*	starve
***pagar** *(tr/intr)*	pay, pay for **7**
pagar un depósito	pay a deposit
pagar y marcharse	check out
palear *(tr)*	paddle (*boat*) **2**
palidecer *(intr)*	turn pale **32**
palpar *(tr)*	feel, caress, touch **2**
palpitar *(intr)*	pound, palpitate, beat **2**
paralizar *(tr)*	paralyze **6**
parar(se) *(tr/refl)*	stop; draw up, stall; turn off (*engine*) **2**
parecer *(intr)*	appear, seem, look (like) **32**
parecerse a *(refl)*	take after, resemble **32**
parpadear *(intr)*	blink; wink, flicker, twinkle **2**
participar *(intr)*	participate, take part, join in, share **2**
partir *(intr)*	leave, depart; start out **4**
partir en dos *(tr)*	halve
partir por mitad *(tr)*	halve, separate into two
partir(se) *(tr/refl)*	split, share, partition off, divide **4**
pasar *(tr)*	spend (*time*) **2**
pasar por *(intr)*	pass; go through; happen; wear off
pasar a cuenta nueva *(tr)*	carry forward
pasar cerca de *(intr)*	pass, pass by
pasar de largo *(intr)*	bypass
pasar de moda *(intr)*	go out of fashion
pasar hambre *(intr)*	starve
pasar inadvertido *(intr)*	slip by unnoticed
pasar la aspiradora *(tr)*	vacuum
pasar la noche *(intr)*	have a good time
pasar por una criba *(tr)*	screen, sift
pasarse sin *(tr)*	do without **2**
pasear(se) *(tr/intr/refl)*	go for a walk, take for a walk, walk (e.g. *dog*), ramble, stroll **2**
pasmar *(tr)*	dumbfound, stupefy **2**
pastar *(tr/intr)*	graze **2**
patear *(tr/intr)*	stamp (*foot*) **2**
patentar *(tr)*	patent **2**
patinar *(intr)*	skate **2**
pavimentar *(tr)*	pave **2**
pecar *(tr)*	sin **5**

pedalear *(intr)*	pedal **2**
***pedir** *(tr)*	ask for, request, beg; charge (*price*), ask someone to do something; require, order **24**
pedir perdón *(intr)*	say sorry, apologize
pedir prestado *(tr)*	borrow
pegar *(tr)*	glue; hang (*wallpaper*); hit, beat, punch, slap, smack, strike **7**
pegarse a *(refl)*	adhere to, stick to, cling to **7**
peinar *(tr)*	comb **2**
pelar *(tr)*	peel **2**
pelearse *(refl)*	fight, argue, quarrel, fall out **2**
pellizcar *(tr)*	pinch **5**
pender *(intr)*	hang **3**
penetrar *(tr)*	penetrate; see through **2**
***pensar** *(tr/intr)*	think, believe; intend **19**
pensar en *(tr)*	think of
pensionar *(tr)*	pension **2**
percibir *(tr)*	discern, perceive, sense **4**
perder *(tr/intr)*	lose **19**
perder el conocimiento *(intr)*	pass out, faint
perder el tiempo *(intr)*	lose time, loiter
perder la paciencia *(intr)*	lose one's temper
perderse *(refl)*	get lost, stray **19**
perdonar *(tr)*	pardon, forgive, let off, spare (*life*) **2**
perdurar *(intr)*	stand, remain unchanged **2**
perecer *(intr)*	perish **32**
perfeccionar(se) *tr/refl)*	perfect, improve **2**
perfilar *(tr)*	outline **2**
perforar *(tr)*	perforate; drill; sink (*well*) **2**
perfumar *(tr)*	perfume, scent **2**
perjudicar *(tr)*	damage, harm, handicap **5**
permanecer *(intr)*	remain, stay **32**
permitir *(tr)*	permit, allow, let **4**
pernoctar *(intr)*	stop over, stay the night **2**
perpetuar *(tr)*	perpetuate **15**
perseguir *(tr/intr)*	pursue, hound, chase, follow **10**

persistir *(intr)*	persist, keep on, keep at, stick to **4**
persuadir *(tr)*	persuade **4**
pertenecer *(intr)*	belong **32**
perturbar *(tr)*	disturb **2**
pesar *(tr/intr)*	weigh **2**
pescar *(tr)*	fish **5**
pestañear *(intr)*	blink, wink **2**
picar *(tr)*	stick, prick, sting itch; mince (*food*) **5**
picotear *(tr/intr)*	peck, peck at **2**
pillar *(tr)*	pillage; seize; catch, catch out **2**
pilotar *(tr)*	pilot, fly **2**
pinchar *(tr)*	prick **2**
pintar *(tr/intr)*	paint, depict **2**
pisar *(tr/intr)*	step, tread **2**
pisotear *(tr)*	tread, trample **2**
planchar *(tr)*	iron **2**
planear *(tr/intr)*	glide, plan **2**
planificar *(tr)*	plan **5**
plantar *(tr)*	plant **2**
platear *(tr)*	silver **2**
platicar *(intr)*	talk, chat **5**
plegar(se) *(tr/refl)*	fold, fold up, pleat; wrinkle, crease **7, 19**
plisar *(tr)*	pleat **2**
podar *(tr)*	prune **2**
***poder** *(intr)*	be able (to), can, may (*in requests*, etc.) **46**
poder con *(intr)*	cope with
polucionar *(tr)*	pollute **2**
polvorear *(tr)*	powder **2**
***poner** *(tr)*	place, put, put in, stick; turn on, switch on **47**
poner a flotar *(tr)*	float
poner al revés *(tr)*	turn inside out
poner del revés	turn upside down
poner en libertad *(tr)*	free, set free
poner en obra *(tr)*	put into practice
poner en orden *(tr)*	put in order; tidy, tidy up
poner en una lista *(tr)*	list
poner guarniciones a *(tr)*	harness
poner huevos *(tr)*	lay eggs
poner la mesa	lay (*table*)
poner las esposas a *(tr)*	handcuff

preservar *(tr)*	preserve **2**
presidir *(tr/intr)*	preside, chair **4**
presionar *(tr)*	depress, push down, press (*button*, etc.) **2**
prestar *(tr)*	lend **2**
prestar atención *(intr)*	attend, pay attention
presupuestar *(tr)*	budget **2**
pretender *(tr)*	pretend; claim **3**
prevenir *(tr)*	prevent, warn **57**
prever *(tr)*	foresee, forecast **58**
privar de *(tr)*	deprive, do out of **2**
privar de comida *(tr)*	starve
privatizar *(tr)*	privatize **6**
probar(se) *(tr/intr/refl)*	try, test, try on, try out; prove, show; sample, taste **20**
proceder de *(intr)*	proceed, come from, derive from **3**
procesar *(tr)*	try, prosecute, word process **2**
procrear *(tr)*	procreate **2**
producir *(tr)*	produce, generate, yield **31**
profundizar *(tr)*	deepen **6**
programar *(tr)*	program **2**
progresar *(intr)*	progress **2**
prohibir *(tr)*	prohibit, forbid **15**
prolongar *(tr)*	prolong, extend **7**
prometer *(tr)*	promise **3**
prometerse *(refl)*	get engaged **3**
promocionar *(tr)*	promote **2**
promover *(tr)*	promote **20**
pronosticar *(tr)*	predict, forecast **5**
pronunciar *(tr)*	pronounce **2**
pronunciar un discurso *(tr)*	speak (*deliver speech*)
propagar *(tr)*	spread **7**
proponer(se) *(tr/refl)*	propose; intend to do **47**
proporcionar *(tr)*	provide, afford, supply, furnish **2**
prorratear *(tr)*	average **2**
proseguir *(tr/intr)*	prosecute; get on with (it) **10**
prosperar *(tr)*	thrive, prosper **2**
prostituirse *(refl)*	prostitute oneself **12**
proteger *(tr)*	guard, protect **11**
protestar *(tr/intr)*	protest **2**

proveer de *(tr)* — provide, furnish, stock, supply, equip with **13**
  proveer de personal *(tr)* — staff
provenir de *(tr)* — come from, derive from **57**
provocar *(tr)* — trigger, trigger off, provoke **5**
proyectar *(tr)* — plan, project; hurl, throw; scheme **2**
publicar *(tr)* — publicize; publish, bring out **5**
pudrir(se) *(tr/refl)* — rot, decay **4**
pulir *(tr)* — polish **4**
pulsar *(tr)* — press (*button*, etc.) **2**
pulverizar(se) *(tr/refl)* — pulverize, powder **6**
purificar *(tr)* — refine, purify **5**

Q

quebrar(se) *(tr/refl)* — break, smash **19**
quedar *(intr)* — remain, stay **2**
  quedar en pie *(intr)* — stand, remain standing
  quedar en *(tr)* — decide on
  quedar sin *(tr)* — run out of
quedar(se) *(refl)* — stay, remain, stay behind **2**
  quedarse atrás — drop back
  quedarse dormido *(intr)* — fall asleep, nod off
quejar(se) *(intr/refl)* — complain, groan, grumble, moan **2**
***querer** *(tr)* — want, wish, like, love **48**
  querer *(+ infinitive)* — mean to do something
  querer decir *(tr)* — mean
quitar(se) *(tr/refl)* — take off; clear away; turn off, switch off; turn out; withdraw; take off (*clothes*); wear off, remove, take away **2**
  quitar con un trapo *(tr)* — wipe off
  quitar el polvo *(tr)* — dust

R

racionar *(tr)* — ration **2**
radiografiar *(tr)* — x-ray **14**
raer *(tr)* — scrape **30**
rajar(se) *(tr/refl)* — split; expel **2**
rallar *(tr)* — grate **2**
raptar *(tr)* — kidnap **2**
rascar(se) *(tr/refl)* — scratch **5**

rasgar(se) *(tr/refl)*	tear **7**
rasguñar *(tr/intr)*	scratch **2**
raspar *(tr)*	scrape **2**
rastrear *(tr)*	track, trail **2**
rastrillar *(tr)*	rake **2**
ratificar *(tr)*	ratify, endorse **5**
rayar *(tr)*	rule (*paper*) **2**
razonar *(intr)*	reason, give reasons **2**
reaccionar *(tr)*	react **2**
realizar *(tr)*	carry out, perform; fulfil, realize, make real; complete, achieve **6**
reasegurar *(tr)*	underwrite **2**
rebajar(se) *(tr/refl)*	lower, reduce, cut back, cut down, knock down, sell cheaply **2**
rebatir *(tr)*	refute **4**
rebelarse contra *(refl)*	revolt against **2**
rebobinar *(tr)*	wind back **2**
rebotar *(intr)*	bounce **2**
recalentar *(tr)*	warm up **2**
recelar de *(tr)*	distrust, suspect **2**
recetar *(tr)*	prescribe **2**
rechazar *(tr)*	refuse, reject; deny, disclaim, turn down **6**
rechinar *(intr)*	creak; overcook, burn **2**
recibir *(tr)*	receive, get **4**
reciclar *(tr)*	recycle **2**
reclamar *(tr/intr)*	demand, claim; protest, complain **2**
reclinarse *(refl)*	lean back on **2**
recobrar *(tr)*	get back, recover **2**
recocer *(tr)*	warm up; overcook **9**
recoger *(tr)*	fetch; call for; gather, pick (up), reap **11**
recomendar *(tr)*	recommend **19**
recompensar *(tr)*	reward, compensate **2**
reconciliar(se) *(tr/refl)*	reconcile, reunite **2**
reconocer *(tr)*	recognize, acknowledge, credit; spot **32**
reconstruir *(tr)*	reconstruct **12**
recordar *(tr)*	remember, recall, remind **20**
recorrer *(tr)*	range over, go through **3**
rectificar *(tr)*	rectify **5**
recuperar *(tr)*	salvage, get back; recover (e.g. *health*) **2**

redactar *(tr)*	draft, draw up, edit, write **2**
redimir *(tr)*	pay off, redeem **4**
redoblar *(tr)*	double **2**
redondear *(tr)*	round up (*figures*) **2**
reducir(se) *(tr/refl)*	lower, reduce, cut back, cut down, slacken, reduce, shrink, shorten **31**
reducir la velocidad *(tr/intr)*	slow down
reducir progresivamente *(tr)*	phase out
reembolsar *(tr)*	refund, reimburse **2**
reemplazar *(tr)*	replace **6**
referirse a *(refl)*	refer to **22**
refinar *(tr)*	refine **2**
reflejar *(tr)*	reflect **2**
reflexionar *(intr)*	reflect, think over **2**
reforzar *(tr)*	reinforce, strengthen, support, shore up **6, 20**
refrenar *(tr)*	stem **2**
refrescar(se) *(tr/refl)*	refresh, freshen **5**
refrigerar *(tr)*	refrigerate **2**
refunfuñar *(intr)*	grumble **2**
refutar *(tr)*	refute **2**
regalar *(tr)*	give away (*as a present*) **2**
regañar *(tr)*	scold, nag **2**
regar *(tr)*	irrigate, spray, water (*plants*) **7, 19**
regatear *(intr)*	bargain, haggle **2**
regentar *(tr)*	boss about **2**
regir *(tr)*	rule, govern **11, 24**
registrar *(tr)*	register, record, chart, enrol; look through, scan, check, search **2**
registrarse *(refl)*	register (*in a hotel*)
reglamentar *(intr)*	regulate, make regulations **2**
regocijar(se) *(tr/refl)*	rejoice **2**
regresar *(intr)*	come/go home/back, return, get back **2**
regular *(tr)*	regulate **2**
regularizar *(tr)*	standardize **6**
rehacer *(tr)*	redo **41**
rehusar *(intr)*	refuse **2**

reinar *(intr)*	rule **2**
reintegrar *(tr)*	refund **2**
reiterar *(tr)*	reiterate, follow up **2**
***reír(se)** *(refl)*	laugh **49**
reírse con una risilla *(refl)*	giggle
relacionarse con *(refl)*	relate to **2**
relajar *(tr/intr)*	relax **2**
relampaguear *(intr)*	flash (lightning) **2**
relatar *(tr)*	report **2**
relinchar *(intr)*	neigh **2**
rellenar *(tr)*	fill, fill up, stuff **2**
relucir *(intr)*	gleam, shine **43**
remar *(intr)*	row (*boat*) **2**
rematar *(tr)*	crown, finish off, cap, put finishing touches to **2**
rematar en punta *(intr)*	taper
remendar *(tr)*	patch **19**
remojar(se) *(tr/refl)*	soak, steep **2**
remolcar *(tr)*	tow, tow away **5**
remontar a *(intr)*	date back to **2**
remontarse *(refl)*	soar **2**
remover *(tr)*	stir **20**
rendir(se) *(tr/refl)*	yield, produce; give up, surrender, capitulate, give in **24**
renovar(se) *(tr/refl)*	renew, renovate **20**
renunciar a *(tr)*	renounce, give up, disclaim, resign **2**
reñir *(intr)*	argue, quarrel, fall out **17, 24**
reorganizar(se) *(tr/refl)*	reorganize **6**
reparar *(tr)*	fix, repair **2**
repartir *(tr)*	distribute, deliver, give out, hand out, share out, pass round **4**
repasar *(tr)*	revise, study again **2**
repetir *(tr)*	repeat, echo; play back **24**
repicar *(intr)*	chime, peal **5**
reponerse *(refl)*	get fit, recover (*health*) **47**
represar *(tr)*	repress, dam **2**
representar *(tr/intr)*	represent; play a role, perform, portray, depict show, put on (*play*), stage; stand for **2**
reprochar *(tr)*	reproach **2**
reproducir(se) *(tr/refl)*	reproduce **31**

repugnar *(tr)*	disgust **2**
requerir *(tr)*	require; call for, summon; want, demand **22**
resbalar *(intr)*	skid, slide **2**
rescatar *(tr)*	rescue **2**
reservar *(tr)*	reserve **2**
resistir *(intr)*	resist, stand up to, oppose; hold out, endure **4**
resollar *(intr)*	pant **2**
resolver *(tr)*	solve, resolve, arbitrate, figure/work out (*solution*) **20**
resolver(se) a *(tr/refl)*	resolve (to), make up one's mind **20**
resonar *(intr)*	blare, resound, echo, sound **20**
respaldar *(tr)*	support, strengthen **2**
respeter *(tr)*	respect **2**
respirar *(intr)*	breathe **2**
respirar con dificultad *(intr)*	gasp
responder *(tr)*	reply **3**
responder de	account for
restar *(tr)*	subtract **2**
restaurar *(tr)*	restore **2**
restregar *(tr)*	rub, scrub **7**
restringir *(tr)*	restrict, limit **11**
resucitar *(tr/intr)*	revive **2**
resultar *(intr)*	turn out, result as, work out **2**
resultar de *(intr)*	result from
resumir *(tr)*	sum up, summarize **4**
retar *(tr)*	challenge **2**
retardar *(tr)*	slow down **2**
retener *(tr)*	keep back, retain, hold back **54**
retirar(se) *(tr/refl)*	retire; cancel; withdraw, take out (*money from bank*, etc.) **2**
retorcer(se) *(tr/refl)*	twist **9**
retransmitir *(tr)*	relay **4**
retrasar *(tr)*	delay **2**
retroceder *(intr)*	stand back, turn back **3**
retumbar *(intr)*	resound, rumble **2**
reunir(se) *(tr/refl)*	put together, join, reunite, rejoin, link up with; collect,

	meet, gather, congregate, flock together, sit (legislative body) **15**
revelar *(tr)*	reveal, disclose, show **2**
reventar *(intr)*	burst, explode, blow up **19**
revestir *(tr)*	coat, cover **24**
revestir de acero *(tr)*	steel
revestir de hormigón *(tr)*	concrete over
revisar *(tr)*	revise, check, check over **2**
revisar cuentas	audit
revolotear *(intr)*	wheel, fly about **2**
revolver *(intr)*	turn around **20**
rezar *(intr)*	pray **6**
ridiculizar *(tr)*	ridicule **6**
rizar *(tr)*	curl **6**
robar *(tr)*	rob, steal, pinch, burglarize/burgle **2**
rociar *(tr)*	spatter, sprinkle **14**
rodar *(intr)*	roll, wheel, bowl; run (*computing*); shoot (*film*) **20**
rodear *(tr)*	circle, surround, close in, encircle, skirt **2**
roer *(tr)*	gnaw **30**
rogar *(tr)*	beg, plead, pray, request **7, 20**
***romper(se)** *(tr/refl)*	break, snap, smash **50**
roncar *(intr)*	snore **5**
ronronear *(intr)*	purr **2**
rozar *(tr)*	brush against, touch **6**
ruborizarse *(refl)*	blush **6**
rugir *(intr)*	roar **11**

S

***saber** *(tr/intr)*	know, know how to, be able to; find out **51**
saborear *(tr)*	savor **2**
***sacar** *(tr)*	take out, get out, withdraw; stick out; draw; book (*tickets*) **5**
sacar con cuchara *(tr)*	scoop
sacar de quicio *(tr)*	madden, irritate
sacar el título (de)	qualify (as)
sacar ganancia (de) *(intr)*	profit, benefit (from)
sacar una foto *(tr)*	take a photograph

saciar *(tr)*	quench **2**
sacrificar *(tr)*	sacrifice **5**
sacudir(se) *(tr/refl)*	rock, shake **4**
salar *(tr)*	salt **2**
saldar *(tr)*	pay off **2**
***salir** *(intr)*	go out, get out, exit, depart, leave; branch off; come out; rise (*sun*, *moon*) **52**
salir a la escena *(intr)*	come on (stage)
salir bien *(intr)*	come out well, succeed
salir mal *(intr)*	turn out badly
salir como un huracán	storm out
salir de *(intr)*	emerge from, get out of
salir del huevo *(intr)*	hatch out
salir violentamente *(intr)*	burst out
salpicar *(tr)*	scatter, spatter, splash, sprinkle **5**
saltar *(intr)*	jump, leap, spring **2**
saludar *(tr)*	greet **2**
salvar *(tr)*	salvage, save (*computing*) **2**
sanar *(tr/intr)*	heal **2**
sangrar *(intr)*	bleed **2**
satisfacer *(tr)*	satisfy **41**
sazonar *(tr)*	season **2**
sazonar con *(tr)*	season, flavor
sazonar con pimienta *(tr)*	pepper
secar(se) *(tr/refl)*	wipe (up), dry (up), dry out **5**
secuestrar *(tr)*	hijack, kidnap **2**
seducir *(tr)*	seduce, lure **31**
segar *(tr)*	mow, reap **7**
seguir *(tr/intr)*	continue, go on; keep (on) . . .ing; come after, follow; accept (*suggestion*) **10, 24**
seguir fiel a *(intr)*	stick to
seleccionar *(tr)*	select, choose, pick **2**
sellar *(tr)*	seal **2**
sembrar *(tr)*	sow, plant **19**
sentar(se) *(tr/refl)*	sit, seat (*someone else*), be seated; suit **19**
sentarse a la mesa *(refl)*	sit at table
sentenciar *(tr)*	sentence **2**
***sentir** *(tr/intr)*	feel, be sorry, regret, sense **22**

señalar *(tr)*	indicate, point (out/to); sign, signal **2**
separar(se) de *(tr/refl)*	separate, disconnect, break off, part; spread out **2**
sepultar *(tr)*	bury **2**
***ser** *(intr)*	be, exist **53**
ser cuestión de *(intr)*	be a matter of, question of
ser de	become of
ser diferente de	be different from
ser escritor *(intr)*	write, be a writer (*career*)
ser la estrella *(intr)*	star
ser miembro de	belong to, be a member of
ser necesario	be necessary
ser operado	have an operation
ser paciente	be patient
ser permitido	be allowed
ser responsable de	be liable for, responsible for
ser socio de	belong to, be a member of
ser valedero	be valid
serrar *(tr)*	saw **19**
servir *(tr)*	serve **24**
servir a uno *(tr)*	wait on
servir para *(intr)*	serve to
servirse *(refl)*	help oneself **24**
servirse de *(refl)*	use, make use of
sesgar *(tr)*	slant, put askew **7**
significar *(tr)*	signify, mean, denote **5**
silbar *(intr)*	whistle; hiss **2**
simular *(tr)*	pretend **2**
sintetizar *(tr)*	synthesize **6**
sintonizar *(intr)*	tune in, tune into **6**
sisar *(tr)*	steal, swipe, pinch **2**
sisear *(intr)*	hiss **2**
sitiar *(tr)*	besiege **2**
situar *(tr)*	place, site, situate **15**
sobornar *(tr)*	bribe **2**
sobrepasar *(tr)*	surpass **2**
sobresalir *(intr)*	jut out, overhang; stand out; bulge **52**
sobresaltar(se) *(tr/refl)*	alarm, frighten, shock, start, startle **2**
sobrevivir *(intr)*	survive, weather **4**
sofocar(se) *(tr/refl)*	suffocate, choke **5**
soldar(se) *(tr/refl)*	weld **20**
soler *(tr)*	be accustomed to **20**
solicitar *(tr)*	beg for, request **2**

		plunge **11**
	suministrar *(tr)*	furnish, supply, provide **2**
	superar *(tr)*	overcome, surpass **2**
	supervisar *(tr)*	supervize **2**
	suplicar *(tr)*	beg, pray **5**
	suplir *(intr)*	stand in for **4**
	suponer *(tr)*	suppose, expect **47**
	suprimir *(tr)*	abolish, excise, suppress, cut out, delete, do away with **4**
	surgir *(intr)*	arise (e.g. *problem*) **11**
	surtir *(tr)*	stock, supply **4**
	suscribir *(intr)*	subscribe **37**
	suspender *(tr)*	suspend, fail (*exam*), call off **3**
	suspirar *(intr)*	sigh **2**
	suspirar por *(intr)*	pine for
	sustituir *(tr)*	replace, substitute, change **12**
	sustraer *(tr)*	subtract **55**
	susurrar *(intr)*	whisper **2**
T	**tachar** *(tr)*	cross out, delete, erase, cut out **2**
	tajar *(tr)*	cut, chop, hack, slice **2**
	taladrar *(tr)*	drill **2**
	tallar *(tr)*	hew **2**
	tambalear(se) *(intr/refl)*	stagger, totter **2**
	tamborilear *(intr)*	drum/patter, (*rain*) **2**
	tamizar *(tr)*	screen, sift, sieve **6**
	tañer *(tr)*	pluck, play (*instrument*) **17**
	tapar *(tr)*	plug, stop, block **2**
	taponar *(tr)*	cork **2**
	tardar *(intr)*	delay, linger **2**
	tartamudear *(intr)*	stammer, stutter **2**
	tasar *(tr)*	appraise, evaluate, price **2**
	techar *(tr)*	put a roof on **2**
	tejer *(tr/intr)*	spin (*wool*), weave **3**
	telefonear *(tr)*	(tele)phone, call **2**
	temblar *(intr)*	tremble, shiver, quiver **19**
	temer *(tr)*	fear, dread **3**
	templar *(tr)*	temper, moderate; tune **2**
	tender(se) *(tr/refl)*	spread, lie, stretch out **19**
	tender a *(intr)*	tend, be likely to

come across **2**

torcer(se) *(tr/refl)* bend (*road*), turn, fork; twist; sprain, pull a muscle; screw, curve **9, 20**

torturar *(tr)* torture **2**

toser *(intr)* cough **3**

tostar *(tr)* toast (*bread*) **20**

tostar(se) *(tr/refl)* tan

trabajar *(intr)* work, labor **2**

trabajar en el jardín *(intr)* garden

traducir *(tr)* translate **31**

***traer** *(tr)* fetch, bring **55**

tragar(se) *(tr/refl)* swallow, gobble, guzzle **7**

traicionar *(tr)* betray **2**

trampear *(tr)* trick, deceive **2**

transcribir *(tr)* transcribe, write out **37**

transferir *(tr)* transfer, convey **22**

transformar *(tr)* transform **2**

transmitir *(tr)* transmit; send on **4**

transportar *(tr)* transport, convey, ship **2**

traquetear *(tr/intr)* rattle; not to stop working **2**

trasladar *(tr)* move **2**

traslapar *(tr)* (over)lap **2**

trasnochar *(intr)* sit up, stay up (*at night*) **2**

traspasar *(tr)* transfer, convey; pierce **2**

trasponer *(tr)* transpose **47**

trasquilar *(tr)* shear **2**

trastornar *(tr)* upset, disturb*(tr)* 2

tratar(se) de *(tr/refl)* deal with, be about; try; treat, process (*data*, etc.) **2**

tratar con *(tr)* deal with (*person*)

tratar de usted *(tr)* address as **usted**

tratar mal *(tr)* maltreat, mistreat

trazar *(tr)* trace, outline, figure/work out (*plan)* **6**

trepar *(tr)* climb **2**

trillar *(tr)* thresh; use a lot **2**

trinar *(intr)* sing (*birds*) **2**

triunfar *(intr)* triumph, overcome, succeed, conquer **2**

trocar por *(tr)* trade, exchange, barter **5**

tronar *(intr)* thunder **20**

tropezar *(intr)* stumble, trip **6, 19**

tropezar con *(tr)* bump into, come across, run into

	turbar *(tr)*	embarrass, trouble **2**
	tutear *(tr)*	address as **tú** **2**
U	**ulular** *(intr)*	hoot **2**
	unir(se) (a) *(tr/refl)*	tie, unite, join, couple **4**
	untar con mantequilla *(tr)*	butter **2**
	usar(se) *(tr/refl)*	use, wear out **2**
	utilizar *(tr)*	use, utilize **6**
V	**vaciar** *(tr)*	empty, clear out, hollow out; dump **14**
	vacilar *(intr)*	hesitate **2**
	vagar *(intr)*	stray, wander **7**
	***valer** *(intr)*	cost, be worth, valid **56**
	valorar *(tr)*	evaluate, assess, price, value **2**
	vaporizar(se) *(tr/refl)*	vaporize **6**
	variar (entre) *(intr)*	vary, range (between) **14**
	velar *(tr/intr)*	veil; sit up (*at night*) **2**
	***vencer** *(tr)*	conquer, defeat, master, defeat, overcome **9**
	vendar *(tr)*	bandage **2**
	vender *(tr)*	sell; trade **3**
	vender a precio barato *(tr)*	sell cheaply
	vender(se) al por menor *(tr/intr)*	retail
	venerar *(tr)*	worship **2**
	***venir** *(intr)*	come **57**
	ventilar *(tr)*	ventilate, air **2**
	***ver** *(tr)*	see **58**
	ver la televisión	watch TV
	verse obligado a	be obliged to
	verificar *(tr)*	verify **5**
	verter(se) *(tr/refl)*	spill, pour; dump, tip **19**
	vestir(se) *(tr/refl)*	dress, clothe, dress oneself, get dressed, put on **24**
	viajar *(tr)*	travel **2**
	viajar a diario *(intr)*	commute
	vibrar *(tr/intr)*	vibrate, tremble **2**
	vigilar *(tr)*	guard, watch, watch over **2**
	vincular *(tr)*	link, bind, bond **2**
	violar *(tr)*	rape **2**

	visitar *(tr)*	visit, come and see **2**
	vislumbrar *(tr)*	glimpse, make out **2**
	***vivir** *(intr)*	live, live through **4**
	vivir de *(tr)*	live on
	volar *(intr)*	fly **20**
	volatilizar(se) *(tr/refl)*	vaporize **6**
	volcar(se) *(tr/refl)*	knock over, turn over, upset, overturn, capsize, tip over, dump (*computing*) **5, 20**
	***volver** *(tr/intr)*	return, go back, come back, get back, turn over (*page*), turn **20**
	volver a cubrir *(tr)*	re-cover
	volver a llamar *(intr)*	call back, telephone back
	volver a traer *(tr)*	bring back
	volver en sí	come round
	volver loco *(tr)*	madden
	volverse *(refl)*	become (*evolve*), turn (e.g. *yellow*), turn around **20**
	volverse atrás *(refl)*	back down, turn back
	vomitar *(intr)*	be sick, vomit **2**
	votar *(tr)*	vote **2**
Z	***zambullirse** *(refl)*	plunge, dive **16**
	zarpar *(tr)*	sail, set sail **2**
	zumbar *(intr)*	hum (*person*), sing, buzz; throw **2**